THINKING
AND
ACTING
LIKE A
CHRISTIAN

*Love the Lord
your God with
all your mind*

D. BRUCE LOCKERBIE

MULTNOMAH
Portland, Oregon 97266

Cover designed by Paul Clark
Edited by Rodney L. Morris

THINKING AND ACTING LIKE A CHRISTIAN
© 1989 by Multnomah Press
Portland, Oregon 97266

Multnomah Press is a ministry of Multnomah School of the Bible, 8435 N.E. Glisan Street, Portland, Oregon 97220.

Printed in the United States of America

Library of Congress Cataloging-In-Publication Data

Lockerbie, D. Bruce.
  Thinking and acting like a Christian / D. Bruce Lockerbie.
    p. cm.
  ISBN 0-88070-289-3
  1. Christian ethics. 2. Evangelicalism. I. Title.
BJ1251.L63 1989
270.8'28—dc19   88-35962
                                           CIP

89 90 91 92 93 94 95 96 97 98 - 10 9 8 7 6 5 4 3 2 1

To Karl and Jean Soderstrom--
colleagues and friends

God be in my head, and in my understanding;
God be in mine eyes, and in my looking;
God be in my mouth, and in my speaking;
God be in my heart, and in my thinking;
God be at mine end, and at my departing.

Sarum Primer, 1558

May the mind of Christ my Saviour
Live in me from day to day,
By His love and power controlling
All I do and say.

Kate B. Wilkinson

CONTENTS

Acknowledgments

This book began as a set of lectures delivered widely, often under the auspices of the Thomas F. Staley Foundation, at schools, colleges, universities, seminaries, conferences, and conventions. A further refining occurred in preparation for the 1985 W. H. Griffith Thomas Lectures at Dallas Theological Seminary and the 1987 Staley Lectures at Multnomah School of the Bible, Portland, Oregon.

I wish to thank the many audiences who have given me the benefit of their careful listening and thoughtful criticism.

I also thank my editor at Multnomah Press, Rod Morris, for his support and insightful critique of my work.

My students and colleagues at The Stony Brook School have honed these ideas through more than thirty years of daily discourse—what the King James Version calls "conversation." The boarding school environment tests anyone professing to think and act according to Christian principles; I am grateful to have lived all my adult years in such a crucible of reality and in loving companionship with my wife Lory.

Introduction

Biblical Christianity is a faith for the whole being. Christians are to love the Lord God with heart, soul, strength, and mind. Such a faith appeals to all dimensions of human experience. To live a thriving, growing, Christian life, we need to develop and mature in each of these dimensions, with a heart for God and others, a spirit for God and his glory in worship, a body committed to God for service. But we also need a mind for God, a mind honed to sharpness, keenly able to discriminate between truth and error; a mind steeped in the Word of God, illumined by its precepts, shaped by its example, submissive to its teachings.

Unlike all of God's other creatures, which act on instinct, we human beings may act or react on account of reason. As beings made in the image of God, we possess the divine attributes of will, intellect, and expression. Like God the Creator, we too can think and speak our mind, putting our wishes into action. Our thoughts may be misguided, our consequent behavior wrong. Certainly because of sin, a human being's rational behavior is naturally marred by selfish motives.

But if wicked thoughts lead to wicked behavior, so too should Christ-like thinking lead to Christ-like behavior. In his letter to believers at Corinth, St. Paul urges them to adopt "the mind of Christ" (1 Corinthians 2:16). He means for them—and us—to begin thinking with the mind of Christ, acting like our Lord; in short, thinking and acting like Christians. Such thinking can and should produce not pious reverie but loving

13

deeds as mind, body, soul, and heart conform to act out what it means to call oneself a Christian.

In the 1950s, Frank E. Gaebelein, founding headmaster of The Stony Brook School, reminded us of an ancient Christian maxim, first enunciated by the apostles and church fathers. In Gaebelein's version it speaks with compact power: "All truth is God's truth." In the 1960s, Harry Blamires called for a rediscovery of "the Christian mind." Subsequently, such writers as Carl F. H. Henry, Arthur Holmes, Nicholas Wolterstorff, and Charles Colson have encouraged a renewal of Christian thinking to prompt Christian action.

Too often Christians have shunned *thinking* at all in favor of *feeling*, contenting themselves with emotionalism borne along by experience, a "feel-good" faith; what J. I. Packer has called "jacuzzi Christianity," based on warm, cozy, comfortable, familiar, complacent emotions, devoid of any thoughtful, intelligent, carefully reasoned faith. We find it most visibly in the distorted teaching of some television evangelists, offering their viewers froth and folly with neither pain nor gain—except, of course, for the evangelists themselves! Such a feeble Christianity naturally can only be a parody of the real thing, as the scandals of television evangelism have revealed.

Yet while biblical Christianity is more than feeling good, it is also more than propositional arguments and systematic theology. Rather, biblical Christianity is a way of life, a way of learning what it means to live out our love for God with all our heart, soul, strength, and mind.

Thinking like a Christian, therefore, is no mere academic abstraction. It calls for personal and practical application: thinking that turns to action, thinking that influences every aspect of living, every dimension of our experience.

The purpose of this book is to encourage a new generation, using Blamires's phrase, to start "thinking Christianly," thinking and acting with the mind of Christ, not just about religious matters but in every area of our lives. To commence and continue thinking and acting like a Christian, one must first acknowledge and experience what St. Paul instructed the Romans: ''Do not conform any longer to the pattern of this world, but be transformed by the renewing of your mind'' (Romans 12:2).

Release from bondage to the world's expectations—renewed and transformed lives. That's what we need if we're ever to experience thinking and acting with the mind of Christ.

PART ONE

BREAKING THE WORLD'S PATTERN

Chapter 1

In But Not Of the World

> *Here we go round the prickly pear*
> *Prickly pear prickly pear*
> *Here we go round the prickly pear*
> *At five o'clock in the morning.*
> T. S. Eliot, "The Hollow Men"

*I*n a Los Angeles suburb, a financial adviser wakens before dawn to be at his office at an hour synchronized with the opening of his firm's Wall Street headquarters, three time zones away. While he sips his coffee, his home computer relays the overnight results from the stock exchanges in Tokyo, Hong Kong, and Sydney; the midday price of gold in Zurich, the value of the dollar in London, the cost of a barrel of oil from the United Arab Emirates. Is it any wonder that as he drives to work his ulcer is already reacting to the day's beginning? If the inevitable earthquake doesn't get him, if the random freeway gunmen don't pick him off, surely the world economy will do him in.

"No man is an island, entire of itself; every man is a piece of the continent, a part of the main." So the seventeenth century poet-priest John Donne wrote. Today, even more than in Donne's age, we know the reality of what Herman Melville termed our "mortal interindebtedness," our inextricable connectedness to each other. We're tied by satellite television communications, by the idolatrous sway of rock music personalities and film stars, by fads in clothing, by slang phrases popularized world- wide, by the passions of international sport, by the computerized transactions on our national stock and currency markets, by the pall of impending planetary destruction through nuclear war.

The time has long since passed when any one of us could hope to escape the incursion of modern civilization. Oh, perhaps for a few more years the wilderness remains unspoiled, but in time the surveyors will arrive to mark the lots, followed soon thereafter by the developers' bulldozers. Urban sprawl replaces the idyllic countryside, bringing with it the congestion, pollution, and crime of the megalopolis. But even before the population swells, a new ethic will have inundated the old, as hospitality to strangers and a concern for the common good yield to suspicion, fear, and self-preservation—all in the name of progress!

In the cities similar changes occur as gentrification drives out old neighbors and the merchants with whom they did business; as community landmarks are razed to make way for glass-and-steel skyscrapers owned by multi-national corporations without a sense of place or communal responsibility; as parks and playgrounds become the domain—the "turf"—of drug dealers and gang warriors; as streets and doorways become home to countless ragged and homeless persons.

And everywhere—in sophisticated New York City, in the swamp towns of Florida, or the cookie-cutter communities of Shopping Mall America—the panic over acquired immune deficiency syndrome, known to every schoolchild as AIDS, has changed the habits of casual flirtation and indiscriminate sex into behavior marked by caution and wariness never anticipated by the moralists of only a generation ago.

Oil embargoes, stock market collapses, epidemic drug addiction, a catastrophic plague: No one is immune from the seismic shockwaves of economic and social disaster reverberating throughout our world.

Meanwhile, where do evangelical Christians stand? What role have those who profess to know the Good News of redemption through Jesus Christ taken to save our world from destruction?

Thank God, some professing believers are involved in the struggle to redeem and restore not only the souls of human beings but also the very planet we all inhabit. Others, however, have retreated to an isolationist manner of living, complete with a vocabulary preserved from the 1940s. But from my perspective as one who travels widely throughout this continent and abroad, most North American evangelical Christians seem oblivious to what's going on around them. A spiritual myopia often afflicts their vision; an attitude of social smugness coats their relations with nonbelievers. Whether by ignorance or misinformation, much of their economic and political decision-making is naive. It's as though many of us—earnest church-going, ministry-supporting saints—had turned off our minds when we claimed salvation through faith in Jesus Christ.

THREE CULTURAL SPHERES

The evangelical church has been reluctant to recognize its true place in the social and political milieu. The fact is, we inhabit three overlapping spheres; we live and move and have our being in each of them at once. Not to identify and accommodate this reality is to perpetuate an isolationism and disconnectedness that has for too long perplexed and weakened the church. Perhaps the diagram on the following page will help to illustrate the description that follows.

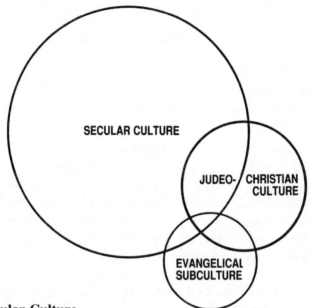

Secular Culture

The first sphere is that world-wide, all-encompassing secular environment called secular culture. Known to the aged apostle John as the *kosmos*, this sphere represents the world and its fraudulent system of values—"the cravings of sinful man, the lust of his eyes and the boasting of what he has and does" (1 John 2:16). Hostile to the Lordship of Jesus Christ, this sphere is ruled by Satan as a usurping and enslaving dictator. Not everyone living within the secular sphere is consciously at war with Christ and in league with Satan; many are simply careless about spiritual concerns, matters they consider irrelevant to the real business of life. Their epitaph, in the words of T. S. Eliot, may well read,

> "Here were a decent godless people:
> Their only monument the asphalt road
> And a thousand lost golf balls."

This is the same sphere described in the early chapters of my book *The Cosmic Center* (Multnomah Press, 1986)—a sphere infected by secular materialism, behaviorism, secular humanism, hedonism, and finally nihilism.

Judeo-Christian Culture

The second sphere encompasses what remains of Christendom. Once Constantinople and Rome defined "East" and "West." Today these terms no longer identify the scope of Christian influence under the control of Eastern orthodoxy or the Roman papacy; instead, they refer to the prevailing political division between the Union of Soviet Socialist Republics and the United States of America—or between the nations of the Warsaw Pact and the North Atlantic Treaty Organization. In political and economic terms this second sphere is simply called "the West."

But throughout the West—the USA, Canada, Latin America, and Western Europe; even in former colonies of the British Empire—another term applies: "Judeo-Christian values." For wherever government and civil order respond to the rule of law, state-sponsored institutions retain socially-acceptable religious vestiges of a Judeo-Christian culture. Even though that culture no longer dominates, the values of the Ten Commandments and the Golden Rule may still be identified and named for their roots in the Jewish and Christian Scriptures. As John Baillie wrote,

> The Christian civilization of the past has not then been a civilization all or even most of whose members had come under such a saving conviction of Christian truth as to work renewal in their inward man, leading them to observe in all things the Christian standards of conduct. It was rather a civilization in which nearly all acknowledged the authority both of that truth and of these standards, accepting in their minds even what

they delayed to take to heart, and trembling when they
were farthest from obeying.

Evangelical Subculture

The third and tiniest sphere connecting with the two
larger circles represents the evangelical Christian subculture,
with its churches, schools, colleges, universities, and seminaries; its conference grounds and retirement colonies; its
overseas mission enterprise; its radio and satellite television
networks; its music and books; its household names familiar
only within this exclusive sphere; its half-dozen national celeb-
rities known outside this circle, some of them notorious for
wrongdoing rather than famous for righteousness' sake; its one
or two world- renowned personages, the mention of whose
name might register some conscious awareness among a random sample of citizens.

Most evangelical Christians live in all three spheres at
once. We're instructed by the example of our Lord and by the
Word of God not to shun being "in the world." We find it
more difficult, however, to avoid being "of the world." Yet, if
we hope to achieve the goal of thinking and acting with the
mind of Christ, we must learn not only how to survive but also
how to transform the world we inhabit.

So in the remaining chapters of Part One we'll look first
at how these three enveloping spheres interact to shape what
too often passes for Christian thought and behavior. Then in
Parts Two and Three, we'll discuss what must be done to break
out of this pattern of conformity, heeding again J. B. Phillips's
version of St. Paul's warning to Christians in the worldliest
city of all time: "Don't let the world around you squeeze you
into its own mold" (Romans 12:2).

Chapter 2

Losing the Need to Believe

As man has gained increasing mastery over nature through science . . . he gradually has lost his sense of helplessness and with it his need to believe in the supernatural. He has become more and more this-worldly and can say, quite readily, "This world is all that there is and it is enough."

Edward Cell

The Secular Sphere

Secular culture envelops us all like a numbing, noxious smog. Its fumes choke the spirit, inhibit imagination, limit our vision. An environment governed almost solely by greed for money and power, popular culture spans the world of government and politics, business and finance, education and religion, entertainment and recreation, the arts and media of communication. It sets the fashions we adopt this year only to throw away next season. Its standards, the values by which we measure the lifestyles of the rich and famous, are utterly transient, expendable, ultimately devalued by their own hype. The result is often a sense of having arrived just when the party's over. What's left for us is little more than the daily grind, the caged guinea pig on his treadmill, a ritual dance around the prickly pear.

"The mass of men lead lives of quiet desperation," Henry David Thoreau noted. One reason for the frustration and seeming futility so many people endure is their certainty that nothing seems certain. Death and taxes, yes; little else. The supernatural has given way to the natural. Our era, disdainful of anything other than tangible, empirical evidence, adopts its new articles of faith, called "the scientific method." We need countless polls, statistics, graphs, trendlines, and computer-generated projections before we accept what our grandparents might have acknowledged as common sense.

The Predominance of Naturalism

In short, we're the slaves of *secularism*, the doctrine that allows no room for any dimension beyond the natural world as we know it, bounded by space and time. Here-and-now is all that counts. Eternity is a metaphor for an annoyingly long delay; heaven is an orgasm; hell, an Internal Revenue Service audit.

Secular culture is totally preoccupied with the present, totally obsessed by instant gratification through the immediate attainment of materialistic and lustful goals. Power, revenge, domination, speed—these are the components which promise the twin fruits of success: money and sexual prowess. Nobody on Madison Avenue sells virtue or compassion or selfless love. Almost every product marketed by an advertising agency is sold by visual imagery suggesting that this make of car, this brand of deodorant, this analgesic remedy, this beverage, this airline, this credit card, will promote the consumer's ego, elevate her status in business, or guarantee his attractiveness to women.

At its worst, secular culture exhibits a cheap regard for human worth, confirming everything Paul condemns in warning the Christians in Rome. For secularism produces not only such heinous acts as murder and bestiality but also, far more commonly, pride in one's own elevation and contempt for another's fall. So while "getting away with it" may be my goal, playing the spectator or even the voyeur at someone else's "getting caught" is what sells gossip columns and scandal sheets. Paul writes,

> Although they know God's righteous decree that those who do such things deserve death, they not only continue to do these very things but also approve of those who practice them (Romans 1:32).

Christianity Considered Folly

Secularism stubbornly refuses to grant even the most grudging acknowledgment that any dimension exists outside the boundaries of this natural world. Any talk, therefore, of God—whether metaphysical or metaphorical—is folly to the modern secularist. Rather, to the secularist, as Karl Heim has written, God has become "an impossible thought, not framable by the mind."

Of course, like the wary schoolboy who scoffs at ghosts yet whistles while passing a graveyard, some atheists would seem to protest too much. The publications of an organization called Freedom from Religion Foundation, Inc. include *The Born-Again Skeptic's Guide to the Bible*; *The Pillars of Religion: Ignorance, Inadequacy, Indoctrination*; *Why I Am an Atheist*; and its bestseller, *Atheism: The Case Against God*, promoted as "an excellent manual for beginners."

But this kind of atheism is childish when measured against the intensity of secularism rampant today. Secularism means far more than the absence of belief, which may be mere agnosticism, skepticism, or even an unbelieving refusal to believe. Secularism is also more than the opposite of belief, which is *dis*belief. For while disbelief—such as that shown by the Freedom from Religion Foundation—may be an active adversary to faith, inimical in its hostility to faith, such disbelief suffers from a logical handicap: To *disbelieve*, one must first grant the possibility of a reasonable alternative, namely the ability to believe. But secularism has no truck with logic or reasonable alternatives such as this. Secularism no longer troubles itself with contesting against the phantoms and fantasies of faith. For the secularist, there are no reasonable, rational, intelligent grounds for believing.

To a secular mind, only superstition and fear give cause for religious faith. To believe in God is to be a confessing scaredy-cat. Peculiarly in our society, fear of any sort is contemptible. To be accused of being fearful is the one insult no self-respecting modern man or woman can swallow. Our culture is geared to creating bullies rather than cowards. We drive our automobiles aggressively; we shoulder our way to the front of any line; we attend seminars in "assertiveness training"; our music and books laud the attributes of intimidating strength and self- interest. Toughness for its own sake becomes no vice, meekness no virtue. No one wants to be thought weak or dependent. We prefer to give the impression that we are totally in control of our own lives, subject to no one else, responsible to no one else. Certainly not to God.

To an utterly secular man and woman, God has become superfluous, the Scriptures unheeded, the church extinct except as a cultural adornment, a place in which to house relics of an embarrassing past sooner forgotten. Instead, secularism reaches toward a pinnacle where inordinate pride, self-esteem, and smug self-righteousness countermand the gospel's summons to redemption.

THE REMNANTS OF JUDEO-CHRISTIAN INFLUENCE

This is the primary environment we evangelical Christians inhabit—a toxic atmosphere in which we are threatened every day by immoral infection and amoral apathy. Popular culture's highest standard is the egocentric question, "What's in it for me?"

A Vestigial Religiosity

But it would be a distortion to draw the picture entirely in somber tones. Here and there, shafts of light break through, like chiaroscuro in a Dutch painting, reminding us of our religious and moral heritage. The Mayflower Compact, the Declaration of Independence, and other documents once laid the framework of a prevailing ethic in this nation. The Northwest Ordinance of 1787, for example, spoke of the need for schools on the frontier in these terms:

> Religion, morality, and knowledge, being necessary to good government and the happiness of mankind, schools and the means of education shall forever be encouraged.

There are also current and constant reminders that this same moral sensibility persists, even in such an environment of moral squalor—a residual morality seeking to sustain itself in hope of achieving some redeeming value to life. For example, each Christmas Eve, since 1949, *The Wall Street Journal* has published its editorial, "In Hoc Anno Domini," attributing both personal liberty and free enterprise to the coming of the One who said, "Render unto Caesar the things which are Caesar's and unto God the things that are God's."

Throughout Western nations, reminders of what was once "a Christian civilization" persist: in the ceremonies marking the royal opening of Parliament or the inauguration of the president; in domestic life rituals, from proclaiming the banns of marriage to the burial service; in our seasonal celebrations, from the First Sunday in Advent to Thanksgiving Day; in the names of cities, towns, and villages; in the few remaining "blue laws" forbidding Sunday commerce; in an athlete's pausing for public prayer after a match or upon scoring a touchdown; in the thousands of business people who leave work to attend a nearby church for part of the three-hour observance on Good Friday; in centuries-old music and paintings still performed or exhibited as major works of art. These few examples suggest that Christendom's imprint upon our cultures hasn't entirely faded.

What is this vestigial religiosity? Of what does it consist? Professor Lawrence Cremin of Teachers College refers to an American social phenomenon he identifies as "a united front" sharing "a sameness of views" derived from the Bible—a Judeo-Christian *paideia* or culture. The shadow of this "united front" remains, however shaken its "sameness of views" may be from time to time. This shadow reminds us all of what was formerly a common experience: religious values established by the Ten Commandments and the Golden Rule, communicated largely through the classrooms of North America's public schools.

Today, of course, much of that schoolhouse piety has been eliminated by cries for "pluralism" and the presumed impossibility of setting forth any agreed community standards of behavior based on morality. "Whose morality?" becomes the red-herring question, as if civilized society had evolved free from any common root in religious and moral principles. Still, our politicians never fail to invoke the Almighty, and the Pledge of Allegiance still commits those reciting it to affirm "one nation, under God."

Civil Religion a Harmful Distortion

In its milder form, such language passes along Cremin's "united front" and "sameness of views" in what we call the Judeo-Christian ethic. Its more extreme manifestation we know as "civil religion." Beyond national pride, beyond patriotism, beyond "my country, right or wrong" lies civil religion, a chauvinistic blurring of faith with divine favoritism. Civil religion equates God with the state and—depending on the agenda of the political party in power—the will of God with the party platform. By the tenets of civil religion, we are a great people, not because we have humbled ourselves before

God in repentance, but because we have been singled out for greatness. All other nations, therefore, must be subordinate to us by God's own design. How readily, thereafter, the colors of heaven become red, white, and blue! The anthem sung around the Throne rings with pleasant familiarity to our nationalistic ears!

The chief danger inherent in civil religion is idolatry, the worship of a state and its symbols rather than the worship of the God to whom all nations are as but a drop in a bucket. A second and no less dangerous threat from civil religion is the cynicism and power lust that soon smears itself over any patina of national piety. For the creed of civil religion soon changes from "Love thy neighbor" to "Might is right."

Nearing the close of the twentieth century, glimmerings of the Judeo-Christian culture continue to flicker, even in a hostile setting, and civil religion appears to be surviving.

THE COLLAPSE OF CHRISTENDOM AIDED BY APOSTASY IN THE CHURCH

Yet for all of secularism's antipathy toward supernaturalism, its greatest allies in the war on Christendom have not been atheistic scientists or godless political and psychological theorists. Darwin, Huxley, Marx, and Freud in their day—Madalyn Murray O'Hair in ours—contributed little more to the collapse of Christendom than did liberal-thinking "modernist" theologians and preachers, seminary professors and denominational executives, clergy and laity alike who, in Eliot's phrase, "took the Faith for granted," and sold it cheaply for their own mess of pottage: presumed academic and scientific respectability, social and political conformity, ecumenicity at all costs.

The result throughout much of the West has been the disintegration of the Judeo-Christian ethic and the collapse of Christendom, signaled by empty if not closed churches. In

England, where the House of Commons sets the Church of England clergy's salary scale, where "Religious Education" is a required class in schools, fewer than 3 percent of the populace attend worship services regularly. Let's accompany the British journalist David Pryce-Jones to Hereford Cathedral. While showing the cathedral to a pair of foreign guests, they stumbled upon a service in progress and were rebuked by the vicar. "Not a single worshipper, apart from the vicar, was present in that great nave," writes Pryce-Jones. "Evensong was taking place in a vacuum: *Nunc Dimittis*, indeed."

In an ironically similar context—in a state which both controls its established church and subjects confessing Christians to risking their livelihood and personal freedom—Aleksandr Solzhenitsyn poses this question to the Russian Orthodox Patriarch of Moscow:

> Will we be able to reinstate within ourselves at least some of the traces of Christianity, or shall we lose them completely and surrender ourselves to the calculations of self-preservation and profit?

Even as a result of *glasnost* and *perestroika*, one hardly dares to hope that the answer to his questions might be positive.

By this time, we've grown accustomed to the apostasy of state religion—an Anglican bishop's reference to the Resurrection as "a conjuring act with bones"; a Roman Catholic prelate's serving as a cabinet member of a Marxist government. In North America, where civil religion continues its pretense, we're no longer shocked by such incongruities as so-called theologians putting themselves out of business by alleging the death of God. Borrowing from Friedrich Nietzsche, they've written God's premature obituary—or at least the death notice of a caricature of God as Grandfather-on-a-Throne or the vindictive Old Man Upstairs.

Other church leaders, themselves sheep without a Shepherd, corrupt their role as pastors to become propagandists on behalf of patent heresy. Some bishops of my own Episcopal Church call for sanctifying rites of marriage for homosexual couples; a revised Methodist hymnal eliminates some of Charles Wesley's own hymns as no longer appropriate to modern sensibilities; the United Church of Christ fulfills Flannery O'Conner's parody of "a Church of Christ without Christ" when it contemplates merger with the Trinity-denying Unitarian/Universalist churches; or Presbyterians ordain an avowed lesbian and appoint her as pastor of a cowering congregation dominated by militant women.

Even among persons of more orthodox Christian profession, we find many looking for ways to accommodate religion to the spirit of the times, the language of the day. The greatest scandal for many modern churchgoers would be to suggest that hallowed precepts of American democracy might somehow need to take second place to the more exclusive stipulations of the Bible. Impossible! Unthinkable! Impractical! What about everyone's right to his own opinion? What about tolerance and open- mindedness? After all, isn't God's term of office about to expire anyway?

Meanwhile, video evangelists continue to spread their cheery brand of slick-coated Christianity, which David Poling has characterized as "the spiritual babes-in-joyland approach," offering their viewers "an anemic, pablum-coated gospel that passes for the real thing."

In other circles, the Bible stands accused of anthropomorphism and sexism, so a personal God yields to "the numinous," while "God the Father" becomes "the Divine Parent." The Logos of John 1 is depersonalized into "a cosmic disclosure." Gradually, in these churches, the atoning death of Jesus Christ disintegrates into little more than a pathetic martyrdom or a mythic reenactment of the return of spring.

Is there anything as feeble and pathetic as religious conviction gone awry? Christian profession that has lost its nerve? Especially when that religious cowardice cloaks itself in state-sponsored establishment, politicizes under ecumenical robes, or hides behind the glare of the electronic church's klieg lights? In an attempt to make religion palatable to modern men and women, to remove the Bible's two-edged sharpness and thrust, the institutionalized church de-emphasizes its conflict with sin and concentrates on politics or social reform as a means of salvation.

Few clerics have had the moral fortitude shown by the Roman Catholic Archbishop of New York, John Cardinal O'Connor. In spite of vitriolic political pressure, he stood firm in opposing attempts by the New York City homosexual mob at stampeding the Roman Catholic Church toward approval of homosexual behavior as an "alternative life-style." Instead, Cardinal O'Connor showed his true heart by volunteering himself as a counselor and comforter to victims dying of AIDS. But he did not sell out the church's doctrine for political expediency.

Malcolm Muggeridge recalls an incident which, he says,

> made a deep impression on my mind because it illus-
> trated the basic difficulty I met with when I was editor
> of *Punch*: that the eminent so often say and do things
> which are infinitely more ridiculous than anything you
> can invent for them.

Muggeridge attended a London performance of the musi-cal *Godspell*. Present in that audience was Dr. Arthur Michael Ramsey, then Archbishop of Canterbury. As the show ended and the curtain fell, the Archbishop rose to lead a standing ovation, calling out, "Long live God." No doubt Ramsey's intentions were pure, but as Muggeridge observes, the gesture made no more sense than shouting, "Carry on, eternity!" or "Keep going, infinity!"

It appears that the Archbishop of Canterbury had allowed himself to be overrun by excessive sentimentality. But why this mindless response to so vapid and gutless a thing as

Stephen Schwartz's entertainment? One answer might be because of the vapid and eviscerated theology it represents—a *theo*logy in name only, since it calls into question the transcendence of the very *theos* it presumes to proclaim. If the hierarchy of any ecclesiastical body can demonstrate no more sure foundation for faith than rave reviews for a God limited by time and subject to marquee popularity, is it any wonder that so many people today regard religion as a joke? No wonder so many people are turning instead to material possessions, if not to drugs and other forms of self-destructive entertainment.

The Impotence of the Judeo-Christian Sphere

These vestiges of religiosity are insufficient supports against the adverse winds of secularism, especially given organized religion's documented decline. Jewish leaders themselves admit that 40 percent of nominal Jewish families in America are "non-observant"; they are Jews only insofar as they share the dreadful legacy of the Nazi Holocaust. Similarly, the Roman Catholic Church acknowledges that its schools are closing for lack of nuns, priests, and brothers to staff them. Over the last twenty-five years, mainline Protestant denominations and their most liberal congregations have been declining not only in attendance but also in income and outreach. Meanwhile, some fundamentalist churches, many evangelical churches, and many more charismatic congregations have been adding to their numbers.

To the degree that devout Jews, earnest Roman Catholics, and church-going Protestants think deeply at all about the current state of affairs in their religious institutions, they can only wonder where their Judeo-Christian culture is headed and who is leading it to its demise. Evangelicals may remember and apply Muggeridge's vivid analogy of the unsuspecting frogs, gradually being boiled to death without ever noticing how the environment they inhabit has grown more and more lethal.

At root, the weakness of the Judeo-Christian culture stems from its leaders' desire for social respectability and their willingness to compromise religious teachings in quest of social acceptance. They represent a form of godliness, a religious profession utterly devoid of power and wholeness, ignorant of the relationship between faith and practice, lacking *integration*, lacking the distinctives of biblical authority.

In place of a clear and prophetic voice from the pulpit, America has turned to radio and television psychotherapists and other self-appointed dispensers of the devil's lie: Dr. Ruth Westheimer, Sally Jessy Raphael, Neil Myers, Leo Buscaglia, and their ilk. Once upon a time, religious prophets dared to warn Nineveh and Babylon; today, modern secularistic values impose their own standards for the religious establishment to meet.

What brought about this collapse of Christendom, this shriveling of the Judeo-Christian sphere of influence? Once its moral precepts helped to shape the laws of Western civilization. Like watchmen on the city walls, those precepts stood to preserve all that's best in the civilizations and cultures known by their Judeo-Christian values. Chief among these values was a belief in the human being's unique relationship with God as Creator and Revealer of himself in written word; for Christians, a special revelation of God-in-Christ, Jesus of Nazareth as incarnate deity.

From this knowledge by faith sprang a new hope, bringing dignity to all of life, dissolving even the fear of death; a new regard for men and women, husbands and wives, parents and children, masters and servants, dissolving the old bondage to pride and caste. A new social order evolved in which Jesus Christ was Lord. Wherever this recognition obtained—however dimly—that domain became known as "Christendom." The cultures that came under the saving power of the gospel combined to form "a Christian civilization," a way of life universally recognizing the supremacy of the Christian religion, marked by a consciousness of the Cross, celebrating the Empty Tomb.

All this has now come to an end. Our ''Judeo-Christian heritage,'' our ''sameness of views,'' our ''united front'' has collapsed under the weight of secularism's millstone, smashing the formalities of Christendom—if not of Christianity itself—into broken remnants.

Chapter 3

The Anachronism of Faith

> *There have been three chief phases. . . .*
> *The third phase, in which we are living . . .*
> *is the phase of those who have never heard*
> *the Christian Faith spoken of as anything*
> *but an anachronism.*
>   T. S. Eliot

*E*very so often, a contemporary event slices through the murk of our secular environment like a lightning bolt, illuminating if only for an instant the gloom of disbelief and doubt. Such an event surrounded the unexpected release from a Soviet labor camp of Natan Shcharansky. After years of brutal treatment, including long periods of solitary confinement, the Jewish activist was set free and sent to Israel. But on the day of his deliverance, his prison guards attempted to confiscate a book he was carrying with him. It was a copy of the Psalms. According to the front-page story in *The New York Times*, the tiny Shcharansky flung himself into the snow and refused to continue on his way to freedom. "I said I would not leave the country without the Psalms, which helped me so much. I lay down in the snow and said, 'Not another step.' " Shcharansky added, "I am a Jew. Our religion is not only part of our culture.

39

Without religion I could not have withstood all that I suffered.''

Shcharansky's public declaration of his dependence upon the Book of Psalms encouraged some readers but stunned and embarrassed others. It seemed so quaint, so out of keeping with the times. By his own admission Shcharansky is not an observant Jew, but he had found comfort and strength in reading the Psalms.

No doubt the primary reason that secularism has gutted the vitals of the Judeo-Christian ethic is as simple as this: First, too few of the merely decent, tax-paying, church-going public have ever experienced the power of a life-changing faith which the Bible calls "the good news" or the gospel. Second, too few of them have ever suffered for their beliefs.

If the Judeo-Christian ethic is only civility, conventional behavior, and middle-class morality, then it's nothing but mere religion, a sort of "faith in faith" rather than faith in a holy and transcendent God. The Judeo-Christian ethic becomes a cultural faith—the sort of religiosity one finds prevalent in America's "Bible Belt," the sort that politicians exploit with their generic and canned references to God and religion. Without the energizing power of the gospel, such conventional faith is out-of-date, old-fashioned, a relic of some bygone and largely fictitious period. It is, in fact, an anachronism.

Furthermore, unlike Shcharansky and others, most upright citizens professing their shallow faith have never been faced with the reality of evil in mortal opposition to good. They've never had to stand their ground or fling themselves into the snow. Never have they looked their tormentors in the eye and said, "Not another step." As a consequence, their religious profession is essentially untested, untried, unproved. They remain, at best, only nominally religious until some social pressure—never mind some moral choice—compels a decision one way or the other: either to uphold one's commitment to religious principles or yield in conformity to mass opinion.

Their reason for yielding is that, taken by itself, the Judeo-Christian ethic lacks personal dimension. As Natan Shcharansky said, religion must be something more than just a matter of cultural identity; religion must work when the human spirit faces oppression. Ethics and religion must become a solid biblical faith. That's what the *evangel* or "good news" means.

Yet evangelical Christians have no reason to be smug, for we live in a sphere tangential to yet very much influenced by both the Judeo-Christian and secular spheres. We're a subculture, a tributary apart from the mainstream. We are also deeply rooted in the heritage of the "united front," the lineage of "the sameness of views" represented by the Judeo-Christian culture. At the same time, because of mass communications, easy mobility, state-sponsored education, and all the other elements that flatten out and conform the lives of modern men and women, we can't easily avoid being caught up in the flood of secularistic living. In fact, most of us are little more than a piece of flotsam in the sea of secular thinking and popular culture; an oddity, an artifact from some forgotten shipwreck, a message found in a bottle.

The Ineffectiveness of Evangelical Witness

To be fair, the blame for the wretched condition in which secularism views religion cannot be laid solely at the door of Lambeth Palace or the World Council of Churches headquarters in Geneva. Ludicrous and contemptible expressions of religious sham are not restricted to Anglican archbishops or ecumenical administrators. The evangelical subculture provides more than a few laughable and lamentable moments of its own, most of them from a similar source: the self-governing and unaccountable preachers in flamboyant "ministries"— surely a word now turned sour in the mouth—such as satellite television networks, independent tabernacles, faith-healing roadshows. We all know the most infamous cases: sordid exposés of televangelists as con artists and fornicators, the ingenious charlatanism of a faith healer's "word from the Lord" (courtesy of a hidden earphone through which his wife informed him of specific details with which to astonish the gullible), the sensationalism of a television preacher's threat that God would take his life if millions of dollars weren't received by a certain date.

Even if on a less notorious level, much of the entertainment—it can hardly be called music—that accompanies these same preachers itself suggests the dismal depth to which awe and reverence before God may fall. For example, aren't you appalled by the sound of a congregation's presuming to praise the Lord of the universe in the banalities of "Heavenly Father, I Appreciate You"? Which of us can presume to *appreciate,* evaluate, reckon the worth of our Heavenly Father? Don't we understand the meaning of the words we sing? Don't we care? Or the cacophony and vulgarity of songs such as "Operator, Information, Get Me Jesus on the Line," "He's More than Just a Swearword," "I Got a Feelin' I'm Gonna Be Feelin' that Old-time Feelin' Again," not to mention "Dropkick Me, Jesus, through the Goalposts of Life." These are cause enough for angels to weep.

Nor can we overlook those entrepreneurs with a keen eye for the Top Forty charts as well as the religious market. These pop music specialists aim at having it both ways, crooning the lyrics of a love song and claiming that its eroticism speaks of Jesus' love. *Who* lights up my life? Jesus or that good-looking receptionist at the switchboard? Take your pick. The key to commercial "cross-over" success, of course, lies in keeping the beat strong and the lyrics ambiguous. If you can avoid any outright reference to the Christian message, then a listener can adapt any meaning personally suitable, religious or not. But we still must ask Debby Boone, after all these years, what she means in claiming that her song is addressed to the Lord Jesus Christ. In what Christian setting is it appropriate to declare, "It can't be wrong if it feels so right"? It's difficult to imagine any

Christian husband or wife needing to say those words to each other; it's not hard to imagine an illicit motel liaison in which those words might apply.

Yet advocates of a diluted gospel will contend that St. Paul did the same thing by announcing his intention to become "all things to all men" (1 Corinthians 9:22). Not so! Paul of Tarsus didn't have his eye on the charts or the bottom line. He wasn't ashamed of the gospel, even though he knew that its good news must be preceded by the bad news that all have sinned and fallen short of God's standard. In the presence of kings and governors, priests and philosophers, academics and lawyers, soldiers and slaves, he testified to the truth. He was not disobedient to the heavenly vision that summoned him to his apostleship as a servant of Jesus Christ. Nearing the end of his freedom, Paul could tell the elders of the Ephesian congregation, "I declare to you today that I am innocent of the blood of all men. For I have not hesitated to proclaim to you the whole will of God" (Acts 20:26- 27).

Too few Christians today could be so bold about the claims of our own witness. Not that we share with apostates and heretics their doubts as to the Bible's integrity, authority, and truth, its necessity in being proclaimed, its efficacy in changing individual lives and whole societies in which it's believed. But unlike St. Paul we are *hesitant*—confused by the enormity of our responsibility, dismayed by the opposition to our faith, discouraged by the apparent superficiality and shallowness of so much of professing Christianity. Our tongues are tied, our lips stammering, our faces flushed with embarrassment. In short, we are paralyzed into a state of spiritual ineffectiveness. At the very time when we should be letting our light shine forth, our lamp is smothered under a bushel.

THE EXAMPLE OF A MODERN-DAY PROPHET

Perhaps we require another modern example to encourage us. When authorities in the Soviet Union forcibly removed

Aleksandr Solzhenitsyn from that country, many observers in
the West rejoiced in his exile as a political coup, no more.
These readers of Solzhenitsyn's novels had failed to notice,
perhaps, in *One Day in the Life of Ivan Denisovich*, *The First
Circle*, or *Cancer Ward*, anything deeper than the author's
sardonic amusement over the bumbling stupidities of a bureau-
cracy gagging on its own ineptness.

Somehow these readers had missed the character called
Alyoshka the Baptist, whose Christian testimony illumines the
darkness and warms the bitter chill of a Siberian labor camp;
they'd missed the ironic depicting of Josef Stalin's altogether
Christian upbringing and its ineradicable weight upon his conscience; they'd ignored Solzhenitsyn's searing indictments of a
political system—not for its politics but for its robbing mankind of our highest human priority, to live like creatures made
in the image of God. These readers had misunderstood the
Soviet Union's refusal to permit Solzhenitsyn to accept the
1970 Nobel Prize for Literature, taking it to be a minor domestic squabble rather than seeing it as evidence of the titanic
struggle going on between Truth and The Big Lie.

These same readers may then have been surprised by the
action of the Union of Soviet Writers in expelling
Solzhenitsyn—in effect, stripping him of his power to make a
living as a writer. They must certainly have been astonished by
Solzhenitsyn's decision to expose himself to further danger by
participating in public observances of Holy Communion, in
having his son publicly baptized, and then in castigating the
Patriarch of the Russian Orthodox Church for his failure to
lead the Church in opposition to the demands of the atheistic
state. In his Lenten Letter of 1972, Solzhenitsyn wrote:

> The right to propagate the faith of our fathers has been
> broken, as well as the right of parents to bring up their
> children within the precepts of their own world out-
> look. And you, leaders of the church, have yielded to
> this and condone it by accepting as reliable evidence

of religious freedom the fact that we must place our
defenseless children not into neutral hands but into
those of the most primitive and unscrupulous kind of
atheistic propagandists. . . . A church dictatorially
ruled by atheists is a sight not seen in two thousand
years.

Then Solzhenitsyn struck his most devastating blow at
apostasy:

What sort of reasoning can be used to convince oneself that the consistent destruction of the spirit and
body of the church by atheists is the best means for its
preservation? Preservation for whom? Certainly not
for Christ. Preservation by what means? Falsehood?
But after falsehood—what sort of hands should perform the Eucharist?

Five years earlier, Solzhenitsyn had told the writers'
Union, "No one can bar the road to truth, and to advance its
cause I am prepared to accept even death." Now these declarations of faith made clear that such a death would be, in fact, the
martyrdom of a saint. Like St. Paul, however, Aleksandr Solzhenitsyn was delivered out of the jaws of the lion.

Yet when that deliverance occurred, in the winter of
1974, most Western observers expected Solzhenitsyn to become a mouthpiece for our own propaganda, promoting the
benefits of life in a free democracy. Instead, he followed the
same pattern of truth-telling that had cost him his Soviet
citizenship—and with the same results!

His infrequent public statements have not been well received. A British Broadcasting Corporation interview with
Malcolm Muggeridge and Bernard Levin, his 1978 commencement address at Harvard University, and his 1988
speech accepting the Templeton Prize for Progress in Religion
stand out. In each instance, Solzhenitsyn characterized the
West as infected by a cancerous complacency, lacking moral

integrity, doomed to erosion and downfall by personal and national irresponsibility. Solzhenitsyn never hesitated at naming the cause of this ruinous state as the fact that the nations of the West have forsaken God. Solzhenitsyn was also unsparing in his contempt for ecumenical compromise, accusing the World Council of Churches of conduct which "prostitutes the very soul of Christianity." In his Templeton Prize speech, he castigated his immediate predecessor, Billy Graham, winner of the 1987 award, for naively declaring that he had found no evidence of religious oppression in the Soviet Union.

For his reward, Solzhenitsyn has received what every prophet who dares to utter a doomsday message can expect: He has been vilified by the liberal press, by intellectuals who reject his apocalyptic word, by those who prefer to ascribe to him "self-righteousness" and "ingratitude," rather than accept with sober reality what he has to tell them. In his own country, not even the apparent reforms of Mikhail S. Gorbachev's *perestroika* have been able to crack Soviet censorship. As of this writing, Solzhenitsyn's books remain among those banned by the state as "unsocial and unsocialist."

THE CHRISTIAN'S CALLING

But just perhaps we may also serve as the last reminders of what it means to be Christian in the sense of being committed to the Lordship of Jesus Christ. We may be the only living representation, the metaphor brought to flesh-and-blood reality, of what it means for Christians to be *in* yet not *of* the world.

How will such a difference show itself to a world that, if it cares at all, assumes that we're mere fanatics, lunatics on the Judeo-Christian fringe? The answer lies in those Judeo-Christian values once claimed and proclaimed—an inherent struggle going on between good and evil, right and wrong, truth and error. Modern secularism and idealism are engaged in mortal combat against supernaturalism and the revealed truth Christians recognize in the written Word of God and in the

Incarnation of God-in-Christ in the person of Jesus of Nazareth. This warfare, St. Paul reminds us, is unlike any battle against flesh and blood; instead, it's a battle "against the rulers, against the authorities, against the powers of this dark world and against the spiritual forces of evil in the heavenly realms" (Ephesians 6:12).

The Scriptures make it plain that the consequences of the Fall of Adam and Eve in Eden affect not only the human race and culture but all the rest of creation as well. Each element of life on this planet at least—if not throughout the whole universe, where sin and rebellion may not yet have corrupted—has been made subject to death and decay because of sin. The very fact of a volcanic cataclysm and the shifting plates that result in an earthquake testify to the accuracy of St. Paul's metaphor: "We know that the whole creation has been groaning as in the pains of childbirth right up to the present time" (Romans 8:22).

The apostle describes the universe as waiting "in eager expectation" (Romans 8:19) for its deliverance. Too often, however, Christians behave as if we were hopeless captives in bondage, rather than rightful heirs. Let's never forget that "the earth is the LORD's, and the fullness thereof; the world, and they that dwell therein" (Psalm 24:1-2, KJV). Satan is no more than a usurping prince, an impostor whose claim to rule is invalid. He holds this world hostage, but only temporarily. For a day is coming when, throughout the cosmos, this song goes up:

> "The kingdom of the world has
>   become the kingdom of our
>   Lord and of his Christ,
> and he will reign for ever and ever."
> (Revelation 11:15)

Until that time, a Christian needs to regard himself or herself as a person holding dual citizenship—a citizen of heaven and God's kingdom, indeed; but a citizen of this planet, which is also part of God's kingdom. As such, we are stewards of all God's bounty because, St. Paul tells Timothy, God "richly provides us with everything for our enjoyment" (1 Timothy 6:17). To us, redeemed descendants of Adam and Eve, comes the commission to care for God's creation. To God's sons and daughters, adopted in Christ, comes the mandate to preserve creation, to cultivate and adorn it with "the works of our hands," until our great day of hope is fulfilled, when "the creation itself will be liberated from its bondage to decay and brought into the glorious freedom of the children of God" (Romans 8:21).

What then should be our response to the situation in which we find ourselves—living in three spheres at once: oppressed by the blight of secularism, discouraged by the inadequacy of Judeo-Christian morality, dismayed by the apparent ineffectiveness of evangelical witness?

We need to break out of the secularized mindset that hobbles our pilgrimage as disciples of Jesus Christ. We need a renewed world-and-life view, a radical transformation that changes how we think and act. Once and for all, we need to return to the rigorous exercise of heart, soul, strength, and mind, according to biblical standards. We need to learn St. Paul's criteria for loving God with our whole being: "Whatever is true . . . noble . . . right . . . pure . . . lovely . . . admirable . . . excellent or praiseworthy—think about such things" (Philippians 4:8).

We need to think anew about who God is; we need to act on that transforming truth.

Part Two

Renewed Minds

Chapter 4

The Starting Point

> *The fear of the* LORD *is the beginning*
> *of wisdom;*
> *all who follow his precepts have*
> *good understanding.*
> *To him belongs eternal praise.*
> Psalm 111:10

So then, how do we get started thinking and acting with the mind of Christ?

A world-class woman runner was invited to compete in a road race in Connecticut. On the morning of the race, she drove from New York City, following the directions—or so she thought—given her over the telephone. She got lost, stopped at a gas station, and asked for help. She knew that the race started in the parking lot of a shopping mall. The station attendant also knew of such a race scheduled just up the road and directed her there.

When she arrived she was relieved to see in the parking lot a modest number of runners preparing to compete. Not as many as she'd anticipated; an easier race than she'd been led to expect. She hurried to the registration desk, announced herself, and was surprised by the race officials' excitement at having so renowned an athlete show up for their race. No, they had no record of her entry, but if she'd hurry and put on this number, she could just make it before the gun goes off. She ran and, naturally, she won easily, some four minutes ahead of the first male runner in second place.

Only after the race—when there was no envelope containing her sizable prize and performance money—did she confirm that the event she'd run was not the race to which she'd been invited. That race was being held several miles farther up the road in another town. She'd gone to the wrong starting line, run the wrong course, and missed her chance to win a valuable prize.

THE AUTHENTIC STARTING POINT

To begin thinking and acting like Christians we too must find the authentic starting point. That point cannot be found within ourselves. It lies only in a recognition of the immutable God, Creator and Judge, before whom all nature and human nature must be accountable. The stern pronouncement of this accountability we find in the pages of Holy Scripture, but these are words whose weight we've long borne in our untutored hearts:

> "The fear of the Lord—that is wisdom,
> and to shun evil is understanding."
> > (Job 28:28)

> "The fear of the LORD is the beginning of wisdom."
> > (Psalm 111:10)

> "The fear of the LORD is the beginning of knowledge."
> > (Proverbs 1:7)

Wisdom, Understanding, Knowledge

Wisdom, *understanding*, and *knowledge*: not reason and intuition, not innate goodness. Wisdom, understanding, and knowledge: the goal of all learning, thinking, and acting. The beginning point is our obligatory reverence and awe before God the Father Almighty, maker of heaven and earth. All of life is meant to be engaged in teaching and learning. The quest for knowledge, the search for truth—phrases so familiar as to be cliches of education. But when Christians speak of teaching and learning, thinking and acting, we must avoid all banality, for to speak of wisdom, understanding, knowledge, and truth means, ultimately, to speak of God who is omniscience, God who is truth. Moreover, the God we adore reveals himself to us as Wisdom personified—the Divine Logos, the Eternal Word, "Christ the power of God and the wisdom of God" (1 Corinthians 1:24). To know this wisdom, we must choose to know God in Christ; we must choose wisdom over its alternatives.

The Book of Proverbs dramatizes from the outset the terms of that choice—a choice between wisdom and folly, between understanding and ignorance, order and chaos, truth and falsity, discipline and license, knowledge and stupidity, prudence and indiscretion. To characterize that choice, the playwright of Proverbs draws upon the reality of human passion and the choice a young man or woman must make between love and lust.

The writer shows a father counseling his son, a youth reaching toward adulthood and the responsibilities of making his own decisions. Into his life will come advocates of every kind of wickedness; chief among them, the adulteress, whose "house leads down to death" (Proverbs 2:18). In the drama, her immoral influence is plain enough, but the true nature of the adulteress is revealed by contrasting her with her opposite. For the woman whom the father commends, the woman to whom the father directs his son, is named Wisdom. The adulteress, therefore, must always be the personification of Folly.

Furthermore, as the rest of the Bible makes clear, the one called Wisdom is a representation of the pre-Incarnate *sophia*, "appointed from eternity, from the beginning, before the world began" (Proverbs 8:23), to share with the Sovereign

Lord responsibility for Creation. God the Father wills the world into being; God the Son speaks the cosmos into existence; God the Spirit illumines the universe with the light of love. This Creation, therefore, is the handiwork of Wisdom, the Master-Artist, "filled with delight day after day, . . . rejoicing in his whole world and delighting in mankind" (Proverbs 8:30-31). Why delighting in mankind? Because to the human race alone have been given the attributes of the Trinity: *volition*, the power to will; *communication*, the power to speak; *illumination*, the power to enlighten the mind, to think.

Acknowledging the Source

Thus, to recognize wisdom, to respect understanding and knowledge, we need recognition and respect for the source of all wisdom, understanding, and knowledge. This means reverence for God, awe before the Lord of the universe, worshipful humility before the Judge of all the earth and heavens. Parallel to such reverence for God runs a realization of one's own dependent state. Wonder of wonders! I'm not in charge of the universe! I'm not the center of the cosmos! I control neither the weather nor the metamorphosis of the gypsy moth caterpillar nor the miracle of human love and its fulfillment in the birth of a child. I'm responsible for none of these. Someone Else is responsible, the Sovereign Lord who deigns to invite me to join with others in calling him "Our Father." The formula is clearly stated: God the Father's sovereignty means the human race's dependency. Acknowledging his sovereignty also means the beginning of wisdom, understanding, knowledge, truth, order, discipline, prudence, and discretion; it means "doing what is right and just and fair" (Proverbs 1:3).

By contrast, a contrary formula also becomes clear: Disregard for God produces autonomy in the human spirit, which can lead only to folly, ignorance, falsity, chaos, and licentiousness. Remember that the Psalmist declared, "The fool says in his heart, 'There is no God'" (Psalm 14:1). Atheism is the religion of autonomous man, whose folly is the perversion of wisdom.

But to anyone who acknowledges God as the Source of all wisdom and knowledge, God promises a measure of that resource. The Scriptures tell us that "God gave Solomon wisdom and very great insight, and a breadth of understanding as measureless as the sand on the seashore" (1 Kings 4:29). This wise man produced literature and lyrics; he studied botany, he taught biology, ornithology, herpetology, and ichthyology. He was acquainted with architecture and urban design, with military strategy and foreign diplomacy. If ever one man could say with Sir Francis Bacon, "I have taken all knowledge to be my province," that man was David's son Solomon. Yet, nearing the end of life, he summed up all his learning in these words of counsel: "Fear God and keep his commandments, for this is the whole duty of man" (Ecclesiastes 12:13).

ESSENTIALS FOR THINKING LIKE A CHRISTIAN

"Fear God." This means acknowledge and bow in reverence before God. To begin thinking like a Christian, *we must come in faith*, believing first "that [God] exists and that he rewards those who earnestly seek him" (Hebrews 11:6). The first step requires faith like Abraham's, faith that the unseen God nonetheless exists; the second step requires diligence as we persist in believing. For those who persist, God promises a reward. What is that reward? Confirmation that our quest has not been in vain, that the Scriptures are true, that what the Bible says about God's faithfulness can be relied on as trustworthy; that what the Bible tells us of Jesus Christ can be believed to our soul's eternal good.

The Bible is a book about wisdom, a textbook, a handbook, a manual of instruction, a guide to life's principles. But the Bible is more than a series of moral tales strung together, like Aesop's Fables, as examples of good and bad behavior. The Bible is also preeminently both a window and a mirror.

Through the window we can see the person of Jesus Christ, while in the mirror we see ourselves and our need for his redeeming love and grace.

If we are to begin thinking like a Christian, *we must know what the Bible teaches.* This simple, logical, common-sensical fact has been the glory of Christian education in the past. Sadly, too many Christian schools, colleges, and seminaries have eliminated all but the most minimal diploma requirements in biblical studies. Then these institutions wonder why their students respond sluggishly, if at all, to high-minded talk about "the integration of faith and learning." You can't integrate what you don't know!

The collect or common prayer appointed for the Second Sunday in Advent reminds us of our need to immerse and steep ourselves in the written Word of God, as our primary means of instruction:

> Blessed Lord, who hast caused all holy Scriptures to be written for our learning; Grant that we may in such wise hear them, read, mark, learn, and inwardly digest them, that by patience and comfort of thy holy Word, we may embrace and ever hold fast, the blessed hope of everlasting life, which thou hast given us in our Savior Jesus Christ. Amen.

"Hear . . . read, mark, learn, and inwardly digest." Surely such a pattern for learning must lead to thinking and living out the truths we learn.

Moreover, thinking like a *Christian* must mean, implicitly, *thinking like Jesus Christ.* But before anyone can think like Christ, one must first think *of* and *about* Jesus Christ. What claims are made for Jesus of Nazareth? The paramount question of history is not whether life exists on other planets or whether the Mets or Jets or Nets will win their respective championships. The single most important question ever asked echoes and re-echoes from the ruins of Caesarea Philippi: "Who do you say I am?" (Matthew 16:15); its corollary is this, "What do you think about the Christ?" (Matthew 22:42). *Thinking about Christ*, his identity as "the Son of the living God" (Matthew 16:16), is the only way to think like a Christian. Griffith Thomas was succinctly accurate in entitling his book *Christianity Is Christ*. One cannot be a Christian apart from acknowledging and then submitting to the Lordship of Jesus Christ.

Thereafter, thinking like a Christian must come to mean what St. Paul called for in his Second Letter to the Corinthians: nothing short of all-out war against the sophistry of Satan. St. Paul paints the picture in the most vivid terms possible, comparing thinking like a Christian to *engaging in warfare*. He uses the language of the battlefield—weapons, battering ram and siegeworks, captives—to describe how our thoughts must be won over to Christ. The Apostle writes,

> For though we live in the world, we do not wage war
> as the world does. The weapons we fight with are not
> the weapons of the world. On the contrary, they have
> divine power to demolish strongholds.

Then Paul, the skilled rhetorician, under the inspiration of the Holy Spirit, reaches one of his most lofty levels of expression:

> We demolish arguments and every pretension that sets
> itself up against the knowledge of God, and we take
> captive every thought to make it obedient to Christ
> (2 Corinthians 10:3-5).

Why must Paul be so bold, so aggressive in his use of language? Because he writes at a time and to a people well acquainted with the rhetoric of The Big Lie of a school of philosophers called Sophists.

Remember your high school lessons in Greek mythology? Perhaps the gods and goddesses of Mount Olympus seemed as terrifying to you as they did to Hesiod and Homer.

But even as long as five hundred years before Paul of Tarsus strolled the *agora* of Athens or climbed its *akropolis*, troubled by that city's idolatry and cynical polytheism, Athens had divested itself of any genuine belief in its gods. Under the influence of the Sophists, particularly Protagoras, the young men of Athens had been introduced not only to a new way of arguing—sophistry means "deceptively subtle reasoning in argument"—but also had learned a whole new set of godless propositions. Bernard Knox writes that the Sophists' teaching

> tended inevitably towards the substitution of man for god as the true center of the universe, the true measure of reality; this is what Protagoras meant by his famous phrase, "Man is the measure of all things."

Knox sums up the implications of this declaration:

> The rationalistic scientific mind, seeking an explanation of reality in human terms and assuming that such an explanation is possible and attainable, rejects the concept of God as irrelevant.

So the Sophists took as their creed this off-handed dismissal of theism by Protagoras:

> About the gods, I have no means of knowing whether they exist or do not exist or what their form may be. Many things prevent the attainment of this knowledge, the obscurity of the subject and the fact that man's life is short.

In the middle of the fifth century before Christ, the playwright Sophocles challenged the agnosticism and atheism of the Sophists with his retelling of the Oedipus myth, to show that divine authority may be challenged only at human peril. But by the time St. Paul visited the Grecian city-states, the Greeks had long since ceased to be, in any theistic sense, a believing and religious people; rather, they had become a secular people. Pallas Athena was no longer the goddess of wisdom but the patron economic focus of the city of Athens. So too with Artemis or Diana and her relationship to Ephesus; and so with Aphrodite or Venus, the goddess of erotic love, whose city was Corinth. All talk about the supernatural could be dismissed as superstition, for most Greeks had fallen prey to The Big Lie, the folly that says, "There is no God," except for power, wealth, and sensual pleasure.

Thus, for such an opponent there can be no other weapon than the dynamite of the gospel, capable of razing the specious arguments and theories of Satan. Mere refutation and rebuttal have no weight; pretty speeches prove unconvincing. Paul himself had delivered one of the most perfectly formed examples of classical rhetoric extant, his speech to the Areopagites in Acts 17. Yet its results were mixed at best: sneering rejection, polite demurral, but only a few believers. Years later, therefore, in writing to the church at Corinth, Paul is ready for a different approach. "We demolish arguments," he writes, urging the Corinthians to launch a commando assault on every alien idea, forcibly subjecting each thought to the Lordship of Jesus Christ.

I'm reminded that C. S. Lewis, when engaged in serious dispute with disbelieving colleagues at Oxford or Cambridge, was anything but the jolly and avuncular teller of Narnia tales. He would whirl upon his debating antagonist, bellowing, "I challenge that!" Then, with his remarkably keen gift for analysis, Lewis would proceed to destroy—"demolish," in St. Paul's terms—the strongest objections to Christian faith.

But that was Lewis's mission and style. For most of us, thinking like a Christian requires *adopting the humility of a servant*. There's no place in Christian thinking for arrogance, no room for self-importance. All of us need to hear again the words of John Amos Comenius, the Moravian pastor credited with being "the father of modern education": "God does not call us to heaven asking us smart questions. It is more profitable to know things humbly than to know them proudly." Or this statement by the Christian humanist Nicholas of Cusa: "We then, believers in Christ, are led in *learned ignorance* to the mountain that is Christ" (italics added).

The United Negro College Fund has a slogan: "A mind is a terrible thing to waste." Let's adapt that slogan to state that a Christian's mind is too precious to waste on its own flattery and preening. Instead, we need Christians who are willing to think with the mind of Christ, which means—as St. Paul again informs the Philippians—to disown any attempt at inflating one's own reputation; being willing, instead, to humble oneself and become an obedient servant, even if it means the shame of a cross!

If we begin thinking like a Christian, we scarcely need to fear for the adequacy of our resources. After all, we're assured that "in [Christ] are hidden all the treasures of wisdom and knowledge" (Colossians 2:3). We're further promised access to God's secret wisdom, "the mystery hidden for long ages past, but now revealed and made known through the prophetic writings by the command of the eternal God" (Romans 16:25-26).

So we come full circle, beginning with an acknowledgment of God's sovereignty, ending by being welcomed to share in the very riches of Divine Wisdom, revealed in Jesus Christ. The purpose centers in the person of our Lord. I know of no better way to utter that purpose than to cite my favorite quotation from Desiderius Erasmus: "All studies, philosophy, rhetoric are followed for this one object, that we may know Christ and honor him. This is the end of all learning and eloquence."

For anyone wishing to think like a Christian, the starting point and its goal are one.

Chapter 5

Opening Our Eyes

"Don't be afraid," the prophet answered. "Those who are with us are more than those who are with them." And Elisha prayed, "O LORD, open his eyes so he may see." Then the LORD opened the servant's eyes, and he looked and saw the hills full of horses and chariots of fire. . . .

2 Kings 6:16-17

*P*erhaps you've never spent much time putting together your spiritual experience with the way your mind works. You've never considered them parallel. *Thinking* is something you do primarily on the job, not in your devotional life—not in worship or prayer or singing or listening to a sermon or receiving the Lord's Supper. That's all part of your *spiritual* activity, remote from cause-and-effect or purpose-and-result or other forms of logical analysis and matters of reasoning.

There are many Christians with just such a division in their lives, a great gulf fixed between their spirituality and their intellectuality. These Christians worry that there's something inherently contradictory, inherently equivocal, for instance, in a Christian liberal arts college; something awkward about trying to bring faith and physics, faith and history, faith and sociology, or faith and sculpture, into the same conversation.

Evangelical Christianity—by which I mean authentic, historic, apostolic, orthodox, creedal and confessional biblical faith—is always under attack by the lions of disbelief: naturalistic scientism, secular materialism, hedonism, nihilism. But evangelical Christianity also comes under attack from the presumed lion tamers—fellow Christians with their jaundiced view of the mind and their reluctance to approve of speculative thought.

THE SHACKLES OF LEGALISM

As Christians committed to the authority of Scripture, we need to confront boldly such subversion by fellow believers who would rob us of the gift of God's own attributes—the power to will, the power to reason, the power to express. We need to stand up and oppose legalistic obscurantism, which binds some Christians like grave clothes. We need to release ourselves from a prejudice suspicious of the intellect and wary of the mind.

Legalism means establishing standards for righteousness that exceed the stipulations of God's own grace and redemption. According to legalism, God must have blundered by allowing human freedom; so God now needs help to tighten the reins, to keep men and women in line. Legalism, therefore, is a form of spiritual arrogance that presumes to improve on God's methods for dealing with the human race. Legalists offer God their help by setting up rules and regulations to measure spiritual qualifications. As long as the professing Christian conforms to his legalistic church's particular roster of *do*s and *don't*s, he can earn acceptance by that sect. But by one misstep—whether it's mixed bathing, being seen with a glass of wine on the restaurant table, or daring to ask the question "Why?"—he can just as quickly fall from legalistic favor.

What gives rise to the rigidity and fear that accompany legalism? Why the disdain for intellectual inquiry and the fruits of that inquiry so common in legalistic churches and their educational institutions? I believe there may be two causes, two crippling handicaps.

Legalism's Handicaps

The first handicap is *a fear of God's own freedom and the freedom he gives to his creatures Man and Woman.* Almighty God, who brought the cosmos into being expressly because he wished to do so, has unlimited power, unless he ordains to use that same power to limit himself. This he has chosen to do, trammeling himself, inhibiting himself, forbidding himself the tyrannical urge to thrust his will upon others. Not Adam or Eve, not Lucifer, not even God's well-beloved Son, is compelled to obey. Instead, God risks the possibility of disobedience to gain the rewards of loving obedience. His grace rather than his power compels our adoration. God wants us to be free to love and obey him, but God refuses to dictate our response to that freedom.

This makes the legalist uncomfortable. If he could advise God, his first suggestion would be for God to rid himself of this *grace* business and these opportunities to choose freely between right and wrong. Instead of waiting until the fruit of the tree is available to the disobedient, let's get the angels with their flaming swords on sentry duty *now*!

Such an attitude toward God's gift of freedom easily accommodates the heresy of legalism. This heresy manifests itself most arrogantly in the rules for membership in the Galatian church. To compensate for the presumably insufficient work of Jesus Christ in achieving redemption, the Galatians and their latter-day disciples add on works of their own: circumcision in the form of an index of forbidden pleasures, a list of merely cultural taboos—and always with recourse to fallacious reasoning about "the weaker brother."

On this matter of legalism I point to a critical passage in the Letter to the Galatians—a text never cited by contemporary legalists, never in my hearing exegeted from any pulpit by any fundamentalist preacher: I refer to Galatians 5:12. Having refuted the argument that would compel legalistic adherence to the law of circumcision, a purely cultural means of identifying faith, St. Paul uses language so dramatic and coarse as to leave no doubt of where he stands: "As for those agitators [who would require circumcision as proof of faith], I wish they would go the whole way and emasculate themselves!" As Casey Stengel used to say, "You can look it up!"

If the first crippling handicap facing fundamentalists is a fear of God-granted freedom, the second may be *ignorance concerning language and history*. A knowledge of language— its derivation and historical development, its limitations, its corruptibility through misuse, its power to evoke—and a knowledge of history, the record of God's ways with mankind, are essential to thinking like a Christian. We can't hope to love God with heart, soul, strength, and mind while remaining deliberately ignorant. For an ignorance of language means, inherently, ignorance of history which results in a failure to understand how God has mediated his truth to human experience. God's use of intervening agents to disclose the splendor of his glory to our perception is itself an act of grace. Moses on the mountain and the young Isaiah before the altar were spared from gazing full-face upon God's sublimity. Even in the Incarnation itself, the glory of God lay hidden in the form of an infant, a precocious adolescent, a humble carpenter, an itinerant rabbi, a crucified convict.

Thereafter, the glory of God was transmitted through the lives and writings of humble folk—"not many . . . wise by human standards, not many . . . influential, not many . . . of noble birth" (1 Corinthians 1:26). But by their faith lived out in action, by their speech and correspondence, by their oral accounts of personal experience with Jesus of Nazareth, by their written transcriptions of those accounts, by their hymns to his praise, by their drawings on catacomb walls, by their formal defense arguments before rulers and senators, by their reenactment of the Lord's Supper, by their following their

Lord's example in baptism, by tracts and treatises of personal witness, by solemn pageants and festivals, and also by their faithfulness and responsibility as marriage partners and parents, by their integrity as workers or slaves, by their compassion as employers or overlords, by their concern for the commonweal, by their fulfillment of obligations as citizens— in short, by their demonstration that Jesus Christ's new life had invested itself in every human endeavor, his followers became agents of God's glory.

Yet too many of us growing up in an obscurantist subculture have been taught a butchered history—which may be worse than no history at all. Few of us in fundamentalist homes, churches, and schools learn even the names, never mind the contribution, of Clement, Ignatius, Papias, Polycarp, Justin Martyr, and the rest. We've been allowed the deprivation of assuming that nothing of worth existed between the revelation to St. John on Patmos and the Protestant Reformation. In fact, how many of us suppose that the so-called "Dark Ages" refer to a period properly blamed upon the benighted influence of the Roman Catholic Church? How many of us know otherwise?

THE DANGER OF ANTI-INTELLECTUALISM

One of the exemplary thinking Christians of the twentieth century has been Charles Habib Malik, the Lebanese statesman and scholar. Among his many works are two essential books, *The Two Tasks* and *A Christian Critique of the University.* Listen to Malik:

> It is neither a shame nor a sin to discipline and culti- vate our reason to the utmost; it is a necessity, it is a duty, it is an honor to do so. . . .
>
> The greatest danger besetting American Evangelical Christianity is the danger of anti-intellectualism.

Anti-intellectualism is—or ought to be—a dirty word in the mouth of every thinking Christian. The American historian Richard Hofstadter defined anti-intellectualism as "a resentment and suspicion of the life of the mind and of those who are considered to represent it." If Malik is right—as I regret he may well be—then anti-intellectualism is also an opponent to God's redeeming grace, a foe of every thinking Christian.

Anti-intellectualism despises inquiry into the nature of things, whether searching for the most authentic text of a biblical manuscript or seeking out a biblical answer to a problem of ethics never anticipated by the prophets or apostles. After all, what did Amos know about *in vitro* fertilization? What did Paul of Tarsus know about the colonization of outer space? We may laugh at such questions, but we do well to remember that during the twentieth century, Christians have wrestled with many such questions; often, the anti-intellectual solutions to those problems have not been laudable.

Yes, anti-intellectualism is, at root, the reason why some Christians fear education, fear a reasonable faith. Some years ago, I attended the commencement exercises of an avowedly fundamentalist college. While members of the graduating class crossed the platform to receive their diplomas from the president, the chairman of that college's board of trustees swooped in upon the microphone and, in well-intended earnestness, addressed the audience with this ad-lib: "I want all you parents out there to know that your sons and daughters have had a safe education."

"A *safe* education"? What a self-invalidating phrase! Only someone who misconstrues formal education as a potential threat to the well-being of a learner could utter such a phrase. Perhaps in the revolutionary system of an Islamic fanatic or in the thought-control of an Eastern European labor camp, education may be considered "safe" or "unsafe," but surely not in the environment in which Jesus Christ is Lord!

For even if there could be such a thing as "a safe education," it would surely reveal itself to be no education—no opportunity to be liberated from the shackles of ignorance and superstition, to be set free from the fetters of prejudice and propaganda, to be released from bondage to cant and conventional thinking. Thank God, a second, more recent visit to that same college made it clear that a new administration desires to uphold the revelation of God's truth in the person of Jesus Christ, who is the *Logos*, Incarnate Reason, Divine Wisdom, the Ultimate Source of Truth, the Alpha and Omega of all understanding—in whom are hid and waiting to be found all the treasures of God's wisdom and of human knowledge.

But there are still people who seem to agree with Shakespeare's Julius Caesar, who points the finger and says of his enemy Cassius, "He thinks too much: such men are dangerous." These Christians are afraid that, somehow, in some scientist's lab somewhere, a discovery will be made or alleged that undermines faith. These are pragmatic believers, whose faith is enhanced by material evidence but might just as easily be damaged by contrary evidence. Thus the ongoing interest in tracking down the ruins of Noah's ark or the fascination—recently debunked—with proving that the Shroud of Turin does indeed bear stains of human blood dating to 29 A. D.

So earnest anti-intellectualism is misplaced devotion; it construes as orthodoxy what is really no more than blind dogma. It's misplaced allegiance to ideas presumed to be immutable truth. To put it bluntly, anti-intellectualism is an unintentional but nonetheless egregious insult to an omniscient God. Anti-intellectualism tells God what is and what's not his truth; it limits God from holding in store any truth we haven't yet perceived with human knowledge. Anti-intellectualism fails to acknowledge what John Robinson, the English Pilgrims' pastor—too ill himself to make the Mayflower voyage—told his people: "I am very confident that the Lord hath more truth and light yet to break forth out of his holy word."

Instead of an irrational, unreasoning, and unreasonable dogma as proof of orthodox faith, God asks much more: He requires us to learn wisdom and knowledge; he demands that we practice understanding.

A Christian *Paideia*

For the educated man of the New Testament age, the word that applies is *paideia*, meaning the full exposure of the human being to culture, knowledge of literature, the arts, athletics, ethics, and religious duty. This was the curriculum of Greek education, taught by a *paideutēs*, assisted by a *paidagōgos*, from which we have our English word *pedagogy*. St. Paul knew and used these words, urging his readers to bring up our children in the *paideia* of the Lord, reminding his readers that all Scripture is useful for teaching and *paideia* in righteousness.

What is this Christian *paideia*, this process of training the whole person to think and act like a Christian? It certainly isn't marked by timidity and preconceptions; rather, it's the freedom, granted by a spirit of power and love and self-discipline, to know the truth and its liberating exhilaration. A Christian *paideia* sets us free from narrow-mindedness and parochial bias, free from denominational supposition; free from received opinions and traditional ignorance; free from shackles restraining redeemed intellectual curiosity and sanctified imagination! A Christian *paideia* sets us free to begin thinking and acting like a Christian.

Some years ago, as Staley Lecturer at an evangelical liberal arts college, I was addressing a freshman English class. I read to them from 2 Timothy 4, where the Apostle seems to be instructing his protege to make the best possible use of his classical education—his training in the rhetoric of argument and persuasion—to perform his calling. I was attempting to connect Timothy's *paideia* in the school at Lystra with what those students in a Christian liberal arts college were receiving, hoping to show the need for them to use their own education in the Lord's service.

At the back of the classroom a girl began weeping, then sobbing aloud. Her professor went to comfort her, thinking that perhaps some external matter troubled her. Instead, the girl rose and said to me, "You're just the kind of person my pastor warned me against if I came here!" She'd been counseled against attending the evangelical liberal arts college, in favor of a Bible institute, because—her pastor claimed—the liberal arts college would deflect her from truly learning God's Word. Yes, her pastor had read to her the very same passage in 2 Timothy in his attempt to prove that liberal arts education merely tickles the ears and turns aside to myths.

But that's not the purpose of a Christian education; that's not what a Christian *paideia*, a Christian mind, means. A Christian mind begins with a recognition that Jesus Christ is Lord, that nothing in all of nature or human nature is out of his domain. Once we obtain a vision of the fullness of God's grace and all that he intends for us to enjoy, our homes and churches, schools and businesses, become focal points to make real the presence and power of that Lordship, that grace.

Jesus Christ becomes Lord over the preparation of food and the conversation around the family table; Lord over the decisions concerning family recreation and a family's move to another city. Jesus Christ becomes Lord over the appointment of a new pastor or the election of church officers; Lord over the construction of a new building and the care and feeding of homeless vagrants. Jesus Christ becomes Lord over the acquisition of new books for the college library; Lord over the athletic schedule; Lord over the endowment fund. Jesus Christ becomes Lord over hiring and firing; Lord over each sales call; Lord over the bottom line.

And in each of these domains—home, church, school, or business—acknowledging Jesus Christ's Lordship means a fresh understanding of God's grace: the gift of each day's bread and the blessing of being together as loving family members; the gift of leisure and the gift of providence as a family takes up its new residence; the prospects of a new minister's calling or the blessing of newly energized church officers; the possibilities awaiting completion of a new church building or the joy of reaching out in love to the needy; the benefits of knowledge found in new books, the rigor and discipline found in athletic competition, the promise of God's provision for the future; the discipline to persevere in hard work, the encouragement of knowing that whatever we do, "whether in word or deed," we may "do it all in the name of the Lord Jesus, giving thanks to God the Father through him" (Colossians 3:17).

When Jesus Christ is Lord over every thought, every decision, every act, then Christians will begin to experience the confidence of Elisha the prophet, who told his frightened servant not to fear the forces of evil surrounding them. Elisha knew what we also must know, that "those who are with us are more than those who are with them" (2 Kings 6:16). Then Elisha prayed for the servant's eyes to be opened.

And what did the young man see? The hordes of God's enemies? The Satanic forces of secularism and naturalism? No, he saw what you and I will also see whenever we look beyond appearances to glimpse the reality of God's power: He saw the armies of the Lord of hosts.

Each of us can learn a Christian *paideia*; each of us can become a thinking Christian, living in the center of sanctified hope. Each of us can help to turn our home, our church, our school, our business, into an armory housing God's own chariots of fire. All we need is to have our eyes opened to the wider possibilities of God's grace.

Chapter 6

The Means of Grace,
the Hope of Glory

> *. . . but above all for thine inestimable love*
> *in the redemption of the world by our Lord*
> *Jesus Christ, for the means of grace, and*
> *for the hope of glory.*
>   Book of Common Prayer

*O*ften in worship I join on my knees with others in praying the lofty and compelling words of Thomas Cranmer's 16th century Prayer of General Thanksgiving,

> Almighty God, Father of all mercies, we thine unwor-
> thy servants do give thee most humble and hearty
> thanks for all thy goodness and lovingkindness to us
> and to all men . . .

We have so much for which to be thankful. This prayer reminds us that we owe thanks to Almighty God "for our creation, preservation, and all the blessings of this life." These are the gifts of grace common to all humanity. We're also offered the benefits of God's special grace made known to us "in the redemption of the world by our Lord Jesus Christ."

But once we've received that special grace, as believers in that redemption, we're entitled to experience its daily and ongoing effect. This is what the prayer refers to as "the means of grace" and "the hope of glory." What do these terms mean?

At our conception we were stamped *in imago dei*, in the image of God. However flawed by sin, we nonetheless bear certain resemblances to our Heavenly Father; we share certain attributes with him, characteristics that make us unique in all Creation. Chief among these characteristics must be the breath of God that becomes in us an eternally living soul. No other earthly creature possesses such everlasting perpetuity. But God also endows us with some of his own divine attributes—the powers of volition, expression, and illumination. When God the Creator breathed into man the breath of life, God also gave these channels of access, these means of grace, to tie us to himself and set us free to be human.

Free to enter wholly into all those good things our loving Heavenly Father welcomes us to enjoy. Free to become conscious, thankful recipients of God's bounteous grace, wherever we find it and however it may be mediated to us: as courtesy from a stranger, hospitality from a mere acquaintance, civility from a bureaucrat, sportsmanship from a golfing partner, compassion from an emergency room nurse, diligence from an auto assembly-line worker, not to mention all the other elements of God's grace poured out through the blessings of friendship, the immeasurable wealth of love, the beauty of art and music, as well as the restraining power of God that holds back evil's worst assaults.

True, some Christians would prefer a more narrow view of God's grace, restricting it to the Cross and the Empty Tomb, the church and the Word, special grace unto salvation, what theologians call "salvific grace." Of course, we're not slighting God's redemptive work through the death and resurrection of Jesus Christ; but doesn't thinking like a Christian require us to discover more of God's unstinting grace? Isn't Creation itself and our participation in it evidence enough of grace? Isn't the Incarnation, with its eternal ratifying of human existence, another evidence of grace? And with such evidence, won't we find in the human components of mind, body, soul, and emotions parallels in the experience of our Incarnate Lord?

What about other gifts? Food and drink, love and marriage, birth and family life, shelter and work, recreation and companionship, self-discipline resulting in achievement or even disappointment? Aren't all these elements of life part of what the Apostle James calls "every good and perfect gift" (James 1:17)? How dare we disdain them when, in fact, they come from God, "who richly provides us with everything for our enjoyment" (1 Timothy 6:17)?

Why, then, does God's invitation to enjoy all he offers trouble so many Christians? Because they may still be encumbered by those fetters of legalism we encountered in the previous chapter. Almost every time I speak in these terms, some member of my audience asks in deep sincerity, "But where's the line between liberty and license? How do you keep from going too far?"

The question, while earnest, reveals the depth to which a legalistic attitude has penetrated the spirit, the degree to which the demands of legalism have usurped the biblical offer of freedom in Christ. Drawing lines, establishing boundaries, posting fences, erecting walls: These are all devices to prevent free access. But do they work? Not if a thief chooses to sneak through the fence or climb the wall; not if an aggressor nation chooses to violate a neighboring nation's boundary.

Have you thought about legalism in these terms? Faced by the power of human willfulness, the Law is inept. It can't prevent hatred or lust or envy; it can't forestall murder or rape or theft. Legalists can draw all the lines they want, but to what avail? St. Paul would have called drawing lines another evidence of the Law's ineffectiveness. And if not even the Law of God can keep us from sin, what use are petty rules for church membership?

The same is true for anti-intellectualism. Drawing lines around what Christians may or may not learn is always to circumscribe Christians within a religious vacuum. As thinking Christians, however, we can't afford to cut ourselves off from our own culture and hope to maintain an effective witness to that culture. We're summoned by our Lord to be salt as a preservative against further corruption; we're called to be lights set upon a hill to brighten the whole countryside (Matthew 5:13-16). But to be effective, salt must be rubbed into the meat we wish to preserve; it can't be left in the mines of Utah or standing in its saltcellar on the table. To be effective, a light must shine in the darkness; a streetlamp blazing at high noon is a waste of electricity. To redeem the world we must be a part of that world.

But some Christians preach an unbalanced emphasis upon withdrawal from the world, calling it "separation." They pride themselves on their alienation from their own culture, on their refusal to participate in the entertainments and pleasures of the City of Destruction. Separationists also profess a gospel of contention and strife with other Christians, not on grounds of doctrinal difference but on grounds of practical Christian living, limiting their fellowship by ostracizing less scrupulous believers. Theirs is a sadly deformed version of the Christian life, the very opposite of the abundant life in Christ promised to us.

Please don't misunderstand my point: I believe that the Bible teaches *separateness*; the Bible does not teach *separationism*. What's the difference?

In distinguishing between biblical *separateness* and non-biblical *separationism*, it's clear that the Bible most assuredly calls for *separateness*: The people of God are to live by standards distinctively different from the pagans around them. But biblical *separateness* is something other than *separationism* as it's generally insisted upon in such homes, churches, and schools. *Separateness*, as I'm using that term, is God's mandate for holy living; *separationism* is man's attempt at achieving holiness. It's the old conflict between faith and works, grace and law.

Throughout my childhood and adolescence, I heard a great deal from my father, an independent Baptist preacher, and his colleagues in the pulpit about "separation." I never once heard anything about the biblical command for *integration*! Perhaps the favorite Scripture verse for these preachers was "Come out from among them and be ye separate" (2 Corinthians 6:17 KJV). None of us listening could be in any doubt as to what this verse meant or how it applied to our lives. We had radio preachers and evangelists to inveigh against booze and Hollywood (there was no television in those days), boogie-woogie or "swing and sway with Sammy Kaye." Lucky Strikes and Chesterfields were forbidden, except in Southern churches, where mixed bathing was the most dreaded taboo. One evangelist wrote books about the evils of bobbed hair, bossy wives, and women preachers. We were trained to tell who was and who was not enrolled in the Lamb's Book of Life by whether or not she wore lipstick or he played cards or the church they attended had a Wednesday night prayer meeting or belonged to the ecumenical movement.

We were instructed to shun such persons, not only for fear of defiling ourselves but also to avoid seeming to condone or endorse their behavior. Some of us were also taught to distinguish among several degrees of separation—that is to say, Mr. A may not have fellowship with Mr. B because Mr. B, while a believer himself, associates with Mrs. C, who is a known supporter of questionable causes.

Closer study of God's Word convinces me that this kind of separationism, as proclaimed and practiced by Christians committed to that stance, is neither accurately biblical nor Christ-like. It isn't accurately biblical, first, because authentic biblical *separateness*—as distinct from what I'm calling *separationism*—is always a call to sacrifice, not to prideful self-esteem.

When God summons Israel to separateness, when St. Paul commands his Corinthian readers to separate themselves from idol worshipers, there's a loss to be incurred, a cost to be paid. But there's also a higher objective to be attained, and that objective is primary. Whatever evidence of holiness or "sanctification" there may be doesn't result from an act of sacrifice as some sort of cause-effect consequence; holiness doesn't develop *because of* the act of separating from the unclean element in the camp or in the church. The desire for holiness, the desire to please God, comes *first*; then come the results, and only from God's grace.

Separationism gets the cart before the horse. Separationism supposes that if I avoid this or that sinful pleasure, I'll be living more in tune with God's will. The focus is on *me*, what *I'm* doing to live a more holy life, what *I'm* giving up, the tainted associations *I'm* avoiding. Separationism ignores or distorts the real message of "sanctification"—holy living—which can be only by grace alone. In place of grace, separationism substitutes works, consisting mostly of the avoidance of a specified index. Adherence to this index becomes its own test of purity. The qualifications to serve as a deacon or Sunday School teacher are expanded beyond what the New Testament states to include extrabiblical or even nonbiblical standards to determine whether or not the candidate is living "a separated life"—which means, does he or doesn't he violate any of the provisions on our particular checklist of sins.

Second, separationism is an extreme measure uniformly applied to all cases. Separationism knows nothing of moderation, which is clearly the New Testament standard. Rather, separationism classifies all dancing as lustful, all movies as trash, all consumption of alcoholic beverages as drunkenness, all card playing as gambling, all popular music as defiling, all secular entertainment as sinful; therefore, says the separationist, a Christian may not indulge in any of these practices at any time or to any extent.

Yes, it's true that Jesus warned against looking and lusting; he also recommended an extreme measure to avoid looking at all:

> If your right eye causes you to sin, gouge it out
> and throw it away. It is better for you to lose one part
> of your body than for your whole body to be thrown
> into hell (Matthew 5:29).

But are we to assume that our Lord's words are a normative command? Are we all expected to blind ourselves as a required act of obedience? Or is Jesus simply stretching our imagination to understand more vividly his teaching, that purity of thought goes beyond mere purity of action?

Finally, separationism is the exact opposite of Christ-like behavior. Of all the accusations brought against Jesus of Nazareth by his enemies, the one that sticks—the one incontrovertible charge—is also the most beautiful tribute to his mercy and love: "This man welcomes sinners and eats with them" (Luke 15:2).

The Lord Jesus Christ was a party-goer; indeed, he was falsely accused by some of being a glutton and a drunkard. He certainly frequented the wrong places and met the wrong people— embezzlers, prostitutes, social outcasts of all sorts. The interesting thing about Jesus, however, is that he neither condoned a sinner's sinfulness nor left the sinner to continue in those notorious ways. "Neither do I condemn you," Jesus said to the woman brought before him, "Go now and leave your life of sin" (John 8:11).

Another incident illustrates the same truth. Before indoor plumbing made personal bathing a hygenic convenience, perfumes and spices attempted to cover body odor. Prostitutes were necessarily particular about using such perfumes. Yet Mary Magdalene came to Jesus, carrying the token of her sinful life—the alabaster jar of perfume by whose fragrance she made herself more appealing to men. But as she knelt

before Jesus in recognition of his Lordship, she wept tears of
sorrow. The seventeenth century poet Phineas Fletcher describes the scene in these words:

> Drop, drop, slow tears, and bathe those beauteous feet,
> Which brought from heaven the news and Prince of
>   Peace.
> Cease not, wet eyes, his mercies to entreat;
> To cry for vengeance, sin doth never cease.
> In your deep floods drown all, all faults and fears;
> Nor let his eye see sin, but through my tears.

Then she poured out the very stuff that had made her sin
more easy. With the perfume, she also poured out her sexy
posturing, her seductive glance, her alluring voice—she
poured out the contents of that alabaster jar, and she never
refilled it for those purposes. Instead, she went on to serve
Jesus Christ and announce his resurrection to the world.

For Christians to rob themselves through legalism, anti-
intellectualism, and separationism is a travesty of the gospel. It
amounts to cutting ourselves off from God's gifts of grace,
then elevating such dismembering to a virtue. Legalism, anti-
intellectualism, and separationism affront the very One who is
the Source of all giving. Do we ignore the teaching of the
parable about the great feast and those invited guests who
declined to attend? Does their rudeness cancel the banquet? By
no means! Others are invited in their place, while they're left to
digest only their sour grapes. Let's take seriously God's invitation to the banquet.

Don't mistake my emphasis for lawlessness. I'm no anti-
nomian advocating licentious living; I'm not presuming that
Christians can be oblivious to sin. There are sinful attitudes
and practices that have no place in a life committed to serving
Jesus Christ as Lord; from these we must separate ourselves. I
find it difficult to imagine, for instance, that God's call to
freedom includes the freedom to be a Mafia hit man or a Las
Vegas call-girl. I'm equally convinced, however, that God's

grace ought to dissuade us from gossip-mongering and envy of somebody else's possessions. Now, there's something worth separating from!

Furthermore, I'm quite willing to be utterly specific in naming, for instance, the promoters of Satan-inspired music and their anarchistic message as a paramount evil from which Christians must practice separateness. I'm willing to campaign against the media that disseminate this music and to call out against Christians who refuse to rid themselves and their children—not to mention their dormitories and student unions—of its poison, in just the same way they would purge their homes of dioxin or radon gas or any other lethal contaminant threatening their lives. This music of death is at war with God's gift of life. Its danger cannot be exaggerated. Yes, sin exists, sin defiles, and sin destroys.

But let's separate from sin, not from each other.

The Bible teaches that God's grace is greater than all our sin. So I call upon Christians to live in that grace, for as W. Wilbert Welch, himself an advocate of separationism, has written, if separationism "becomes the central message of our pulpit, we shall soon see evidence among our fundamental believers of spiritual hunger, barrenness, and personal defeat."

Instead of asceticism and deprivation, instead of legalistic separationism and isolationism, instead of withdrawal from our culture, thinking Christians need to reassert our calling to live in *sanctified worldliness*. What do I mean by "sanctified worldliness"? I mean living fully and freely as children of God in wonder and delight at this world he has given us to care for. To lead the Church of Jesus Christ, at the end of the twentieth century, into a fuller understanding of our redemptive mission in the world, we need the example of thinking Christians living in holy obligation and responsibility as citizens of God's kingdom.

We need Christians who know the Source of Truth and can perceive it in both common and special grace: Christians who know and appreciate nature and can communicate that knowledge and appreciation to others; Christians who know and love the arts; Christians who know and enjoy recreation and entertainment; who know and can explain the complexities of a scientific discovery; who know and practice sound business principles; who know and comprehend the relationship between myth and ritual, history and current events, domestic tranquility and social order; Christians who understand that the Gospel transcends race and politics, government and economic systems, and can speak the Word plainly.

In short, we need Christians who know and delight in sharing what they know, thereby extending "the means of grace" to others.

The hymnwriter John Keble expresses beautifully the simplicity of "the means of grace" in these lines:

> If on our daily course our mind
> Be set to hallow all we find,
> New treasures still of countless price
> God will provide for sacrifice.

Keble's poem goes on to speak of "the trivial round, the common task" wherein we may find evidence of grace. If, then, it's true that everyday experiences make up "the means of grace," what is "the hope of glory"? Isn't it the eternal fulfillment which all these good and perfect gifts anticipate? For whatever their joy, each of these gifts is temporal. Today's sumptuous meal won't supply all our future need for nutrition, never mind our desire for delectable taste. It must be followed by tomorrow's nourishment. But in each day's meal—in each single instance of grace—lies a hint of that time and place when we shall never hunger nor thirst again.

Thus regarded, each meal, each day's delight, becomes a sacrament, an outward and visible reminder of that inward and invisible grace called the gift of eternal life. This is "the hope of glory," not a sanctimonious and other-worldly disregard of our present sphere but a joyous celebration of the here-and-now as a foretaste of the everlasting there-and-then. As Emil Brunner reminds us,

> faith in the kingdom and in eternal life does not make men indifferent to the tasks which earthly existence lays upon them. On the contrary, the Christian is summoned to tackle them with special energy, and his faith gives him the power to solve these problems better than he could without faith.

For it's in the performing of each day's "trivial round" and "common task" that we discover the mystery that makes the smallest detail of our lives a means of grace. Surely God is in those details—the same God who is himself our hope of eternal glory in his presence.

Chapter 7

Reclaiming Christian Humanism

> *Whenever we come upon these matters in secular writers, let that admirable light of truth shining in them teach us that the mind of man, though fallen and perverted from its wholeness, is nevertheless clothed and ornamented with God's excellent gifts.*
> John Calvin

*I*f we intend to become thinking Christians, we must also become informed. In my own case, I grew up almost wholly uninformed about church history, particularly the history of pre-Reformation Christianity. I knew nothing of the work in medieval monasteries to preserve and copy the precious manuscripts; nothing of the brave missionaries those monasteries sent out to evangelize the world. In adulthood, although I professed to be a teacher in a Christian school, I'd never heard of Alcuin or Vittorino da Feltre or John Amos Comenius, the Moravian pastor acknowledged to be the "father of modern education." I also knew nothing about the great legacy left us by the Christian humanists of the Renaissance and Reformation.

Becoming informed often begins by overturning a latent bias created by the faulty use and repeated misuse of language.

Sometimes just getting the right context suffices to make the proper adjustment and bring about the needed information. For instance, suppose I ask you about *exercise*. Given no specific context, you must reply, "What sort of exercise are you talking about?" Am I referring to *physical* exercise, such as jogging or aerobics? An *academic* exercise, like commencement or some other convocation? Perhaps a *learning* exercise, like a math drill or a spelling bee? An *emotional* exercise, such as having a good cry to relieve anxiety? Or a *spiritual* exercise, like devotional reading or fasting and prayer? The word *exercise* needs to be modified by an adjective to give it specific relationship and meaning.

So too with the bugaboo word *humanism*, which to most uninformed Christians means "secular humanism," the only kind of humanism they know. To the unthinking, a humanist is a humanist is a humanist. But you can't lump all humanism together and call it names. Just as there are differences between jogging and fasting, so there are differences among the humanisms, of which secular humanism is only one; others to be reckoned include naturalistic humanism, biomedical humanism, ethical humanism, to name only a few. Then there's also Christian or biblical humanism.

Unhappily, there aren't many settings in which we take seriously such niceties as the discriminating use of language. Most of the time we're in such a hurry to say what we think, we're too busy to contemplate even our own words, never mind someone else's. The result is apparent: Sloppy speech restricts the widest use of the word *humanism* to mean attitudes unalterably opposed to supernatural, theistic religion. The nature of our language laziness is such that, once a word has been stolen and its usage misapplied, it seems almost impossible to reclaim that word again.

Here, however, I want to do just that. Will you give me a few pages to try?

THE CASE FOR CHRISTIAN HUMANISM

Admittedly, we haven't heard much about Christian or biblical humanism from our evangelical pulpits. May I add, as an aside, that when I address an audience on an evangelical college campus and ask how many of those students—and faculty—are familiar with "Christian humanism," I often find that half of them think the phrase is an amusing paradox, some kind of silly oxymoron, like "liberal Republican."

A Brief History of Humanism

Early Christians weren't ashamed to borrow the terms and practices of pagan education, as St. Paul did in his Letters. So a curriculum called *studia humanitatis*, the study of the humanities, became common in the earliest medieval universities in preparation for the professions of theology, law, and medicine. Its subjects were languages and literature, the fine arts, history, and philosophy, with only a smattering of science and mathematics. These became known as "the liberal arts," not because of *liberal* politics or *liberal* theology but because their study belonged only to free men.

Christians believe that knowledge of the truth is liberating from ignorance and falsity; but such freedom isn't automatic with knowledge. The great text of John 8:31-32 promises only that our freedom through knowing the truth remains conditional upon our obedience as disciples. To obtain our promised freedom, we must first hold to our Lord's teaching.

What is that teaching? Jesus Christ gave his own capsule when asked concerning the greatest commandment. He replied,

> "Love the Lord your God with all your heart and with all your soul and with all your mind." This is the first and greatest commandment. And the second is like it:

"Love your neighbor as yourself." All the Law and
the Prophets hang on these two commandments (Matthew 22:37-40).

Clearly, Jesus Christ taught that God must be loved with the
whole being, including the mind.

Similarly Paul of Tarsus, himself a scholar, encouraged
his pupil Timothy to use all his intellectual powers, transforming his pagan education in the liberal arts into a Christian
paideia, the better to serve his Christian calling. Paul wasn't
overly concerned that Timothy might have read or seen and
been adulterated by the works of pagan playwrights; what
mattered was that Timothy should remain steadfast in the truth
of what he'd been taught because of the example set by those
who had instructed him: his grandmother Lois, his mother
Eunice, and the Apostle himself. Add to these influences the
authority of the Scriptures, able to make him wise for salvation
through faith in Jesus Christ, and you have the components of a
Christian *paideia*, a Christian liberal arts education, a Christian
humanism.

But in succeeding generations—just as today—
controversy sprang up among Christians as to whether or not
believers should bother to learn the course of study taught in
pagan schools. Among those who advocated such an education
was Justin Martyr. Born around A.D. 100 in Nablus, where
Jesus had met the Samaritan woman at Jacob's well, Justin
Martyr had been a wandering teacher of philosophy before
coming to faith in Christ. As a teacher, he wore the blue robe
belonging to his profession; after his conversion, however,
Justin worried that to continue as a philosophy teacher and
wear the blue robe might compromise his allegiance to the
Christ in whom he now believed.

Yet the more he studied the teachings of the Apostles, the
more he came to understand that the Logos, the Word-made-
flesh, was the very Seed of Truth; that knowing the One who is
Truth complements the truth of literature and philosophy. So

Justin chose to retain the blue robe until his death, around 165. In his school in Rome, in his writings, and in his public testimony before the Senate, Justin Martyr may have been the first Christian to express what we today call "the integration of faith and learning." He wrote, "Whatever has been uttered aright by any man in any place belongs to us Christians." Justin Martyr advocated a Christian *paideia*.

Others followed his example. For instance, during the third century, Clement and Origen in Alexandria taught new believers in a catechism school. But in addition to doctrinal instruction prior to baptism, their novices were also given a fresh understanding of science, literature, and philosophy from a Christian perspective. In the fourth century, the Eastern bishops Basil the Great and Gregory of Nazianzus contended against those who disparaged learning. Gregory called education "the first of our advantages as Christians," urging all to remember St. Paul's desire to capture every thought for Christ.

Continuing this sprint through history, we come to the North African Augustine of Hippo, who lived around A.D. 400. He taught that knowledge of pagan culture and learning is worthwhile for the Christian, provided that such knowledge recognizes its proper source. Believing that Jesus Christ is the great *magister interior*, the inward teacher who reveals truth as we learn from him, Augustine did not have to exclude learning in any sphere. In his handbook for teachers, *On Christian Doctrine*, Augustine wrote, echoing Justin Martyr, "Every good and true Christian should understand that wherever he may find truth, it is his Lord's."

Surely here we have the source of Frank Gaebelein's often-quoted statement, "All truth is God's truth." Here, too, we find the basis for a Christian *paideia* as one of God's gifts of common grace, redeemed from sheer intellectual folly and pride by that same blood which redeems and restores the whole creation. A full and formal education is part of our legacy as thinking Christians.

This legacy may be traced across the centuries and in every culture, for wherever the Cross has been planted, the academy, the college, the university have followed. While this isn't the place to retrace that history in detail, still it's a story worth our knowing: how the rise and fall of Western civilization matches the influence and declining influence of Christian thought upon the system of education. Yet while Christendom has collapsed in the West, the fact is that, even today, throughout the emerging nations of the Third World, many heads of state, foreign diplomats, business and professional leaders received their primary education at mission schools and Bible training colleges before going off to Oxford, Cambridge, or the Sorbonne.

Which brings us again to "Christian humanism." Would it surprise you if I suggest that Paul of Tarsus and Luke the physician would have accepted their places among the Christian humanists, along with the anonymous Greek and Latin hymnwriters or the Roman artists who drew their sketches of the ship and anchor, the shepherd and lamb, on catacomb walls? So would Justin Martyr and Clement and Augustine; so did John Calvin and Martin Luther and Philip Melanchthon and John Knox and the other Reformers.

The Accomplishments of Christian Humanism

The springboard for what became known as "Christian humanism" in Europe was a concern, not for opposing the truth of God with a religion of man, but for balancing spiritual and eternal matters with physical and temporal issues; in other words, achieving a wholeness of personhood with equal regard for both divine and human responsibilities.

Throughout history, as the Bible itself shows, such a balance has always been difficult to maintain. During the Middle Ages in particular, an emphasis upon ascetic spirituality and the merits of self-denial reached its pinnacle. Part of the whole cascading flow of events since then—from the end of the serf system through the Protestant Reformation, from the

abolition of slavery to the struggle for women's dignity—
carries with it the Christian humanist desire to right this imbalance; to see human life as a precious gift to be treasured and
adorned for God's glory.

No doubt there were Renaissance humanists who lost
sight of the Cross as the only balance point, who carried too far
their assertions of human worth apart from God's estimate,
who eventually reveled in the creature more than the Creator.
If so, their sin sorely overcompensated for the frequent error in
the church's teaching, discounting the value of this earthly
existence and of human achievement in this sphere, looking
only toward life after death and its prospects.

We owe another debt to the Christian humanists: By their
proper correction of an other-worldly imbalance, Christian
humanists also eliminated the artificial distinction between
"sacred" and "non-sacred" or "secular" elements of life. So
the Christian humanist and reformer John Calvin reminds us:

> If we regard the Spirit of God as the sole fountain of
> truth, we shall neither reject the truth itself, nor de-
> spise it wherever it shall appear, unless we wish to
> dishonor the Spirit of God. For by holding the gifts of
> the Spirit in slight esteem, we condemn and reproach
> the Spirit himself.

This may all seem simple and straightforward to you and
me today, but it isn't simple to everyone; and it was a radical
departure around 1300, when Dante began writing his epic,
The Divine Comedy, in vernacular Italian rather than the Latin
of scholars and the Roman church; or after 1400, when
Flemish and Italian painters began depicting their religious
themes by means of realistic figures of common people in
familiar domestic settings. Little by little, artists and then
scholars began to make the love and worship of God less
ethereal, less other-worldly, less remote, less dreamy-eyed,
less spiritual, less divine—more human!

Isn't this perfectly in keeping with the Christian gospel itself and with the doctrine of the Incarnation? Didn't God himself choose to divest himself of sublime splendor—"emptying" himself, St. Paul tells the Philippians—to become human? And didn't God, by taking bodily form and substance in Jesus of Nazareth, thereby sanctify the life we know as human beings?

Little of this reality, the mystery of Emmanuel, penetrated the religion that held sway at the end of the Middle Ages. Infant mortality was high and life expectancy short; the serf system bore down heavily upon most people; education was limited to a few. The pre-Reformation church had little to offer in the way of comfort for this life; instead, its eye was fixed on the prospects of life to come, "the Life Everlasting" of the Creed. Human life and human endeavor seemed to count for little when weighed against eternal values. The gospel was being suffocated by too great a reliance upon systematic theology and philosophical argument. There were few if any translations of the Bible in the common European languages; furthermore, until the advent of Johann Gutenberg's printing press, around 1456, access to copies of the Bible was limited, and learning necessarily depended upon rote acceptance, rather than inquiry and discovery for oneself.

But God is at work in the affairs of humanity! Against this bleakness arose a reaction fueled by new developments in widely scattered yet related aspects of European life: a new technology for printing with movable type, a rebirth of scholarship, a desire for personal and political freedom, a growing need to reform the open corruption among the religious hierarchy, and the beginnings of nationalism.

By the middle of the fifteenth century—almost simultaneously with the invention of Gutenberg's press—ancient Greek texts and scholars who could read them were finding their way into Italy, Germany, France, Holland, and England. Here were men who knew not only the pagan poets and philosophers but also the language of the New Testament and the Eastern church fathers. Thereafter, new interest in learning sprang up—we call it the Renaissance—particularly in learning Greek, then Hebrew, and in applying this knowledge of the Bible's original languages to new translations and new studies of the Scriptures themselves.

It's so hard for us, living at a time when television rules our lives and sets our values, to realize that there was ever a time when books had the same power. But so it was in Renaissance Europe, just as two thousand years earlier, in Athenian society, public oratory and debate had determined the highest ethic. The revival of classical literature throughout the West reasserted human and humane values idealized in love sonnets and fine speech, as well as in sculpture and painting. This preoccupation became known as humanism, but it wasn't human anarchy, human autonomy; it was a reaffirmation of the biblical truth that, made in love, all of God's Creation is very good.

Furthermore, humanism led to a breaking of the medieval church's stranglehold on the free expression of faith, for humanism led to the Reformation. In the nominally Christian kingdoms and principalities of sixteenth century Europe, the church might pass its laws compelling baptism and uniform church attendance, but nothing could compel the spirit to believe or the mind to accept as necessary a God propped up by a human prince. Medieval theologians might plod through their constructs of questions and answers, but could their cold, formalistic reasoning warm men's hearts with the love of God? Could their speculations as to how many angels can dance on the head of a pin resolve the guilt and longing for forgiveness? Could men and women learn to see the goodness and grandeur of God in his works of common grace? What of human attempts to glorify God in return? Could art and architecture, poetry and song, reflect anything heavenly in their earthly expression? Could a Christian living in the 1500s learn anything about God from pagan writers of antiquity?

For men like Luther, Melanchthon, Calvin, Knox, and others, the break with the Roman church was much more than just a rejection of the negative; it was also an affirmation of those positive elements in their new-found biblical freedom in Christ. Among these were what Calvin called "human competence in art and science," urging readers of his *Institutes* "not to forget those most excellent benefits of the divine Spirit, which he distributes to whomever he wills, for the common good of mankind."

For his part, Luther regarded the study of languages and literature to be essential forerunners of "pure theology." In fact Luther referred to poets and rhetoricians as "John the Baptists," preparing the way for "a great revelation of the Word of God."

But not all Christian humanists were Protestant reformers. Indeed, the greatest of them—perhaps the greatest scholar in history—was the Dutch Roman Catholic, Desiderius Erasmus of Rotterdam. His accomplishments are more than can be listed here, but among his most significant were his translation of the New Testament, his paraphrases of the Gospels and Epistles, and his call for Bible study by everyone, including women. To my mind his grasp of the comprehensiveness of God's truth was unparalleled.

Erasmus is responsible for some of the most profoundly striking statements I know. For instance:

> I utterly disagree with those who do not want the Holy Scriptures to be read by the uneducated in their own language ... I wish that every little woman would read the Gospel and the Epistles of Paul. And I wish these were translated into each and every language, so that they might be read and understood not only by Scots and Irishmen, but also by Turks and Saracens. ... I hope the farmer may sing snatches of Scripture at his plough, that the weaver may hum bits of Scripture to the tune of his shuttle, that the traveler may lighten the

weariness of his journey with stories from
Scripture. . . .

People say to me, How can scholarly knowledge facil-
itate the understanding of Holy Scripture? My answer
is, How does ignorance contribute to it? . . .

Only a few can be scholars, but there is no one who
cannot be a Christian. . . .

To be a schoolmaster is next to being a king. Do you
count it mean employment to imbue the minds of
young people with the love of Christ and the best of
literature and to return them to their country honest
and virtuous men? In the opinion of fools it is a
humble task, but in fact it is the noblest of occupa-
tions. . . .

And this statement, already quoted, which I carry with
me as a personal motto:

All studies, philosophy, rhetoric are followed for this
one object, that we may know Christ and honor him.
This is the end of all learning and eloquence.

The commitment of Erasmus to a program of studies so
single-mindedly Christ-centered sets him and other Christian
humanists among the forerunners in the integration of faith
with all of living and learning. Their sense of wholeness in
studies and teaching, in art and science, in politics and government, in morals and manners, in love and play, provides a
model for us today, whose Christianity must become what J. I.
Packer and Thomas Howard call "the true humanism."

Not that Erasmus and the rest were perfect; they were
flawed human beings, like you and me. Erasmus, for instance,
fought bitterly with Luther over his break with the Roman
Church. He complained that Luther "threw the apple of dis-
cord into the world." For his part, Luther had few compli-
ments to pay Erasmus in return! Even so, they left us a
precious legacy.

Christian Humanism Reclaimed

But in our time we appear to have lost our claim to their breadth of cultural and biblical integration. Instead, we've become victims of narrow and defensive views of truth. Now, as never before, we need to liberate our minds and hearts—our intellects and emotions—from all that would enslave us; we need to become open and free to all that's reasonable and lovely, orderly and inspiring, stimulating to further knowledge and at the same time overwhelming in its awesome mystery. We need to reclaim for God what he has given and we've squandered, offering back to him what our hands and minds find to do. We need to commit ourselves to a renewal of that spirit of Christian humanism exemplified by saints and singers, apostles and artists, prophets and poets since Pentecost.

How can we begin to reclaim the legacy of Erasmus, Calvin, Luther, and other Christian humanists, who lived life for no other purpose than to "know Christ and honor him"? We can— indeed, we must—begin by agreeing with them on the importance of all knowledge, all learning, in equipping us to understand and cherish God's Creation. Only so will we be able, as John Henry Newman, another Roman Catholic and Christian humanist, urged,

> to open the mind, to correct it, to define it, to enable it
> to know, and to digest, master, rule, and use its knowl-
> edge, to give it power over its own faculties, applica-
> tion, flexibility, method, critical exactness, sagacity,
> resource, address, eloquent expression.

But equally with Calvin and Luther we must agree with Erasmus and his emphasis upon reading and studying the Scriptures. The shameful fact is that, throughout evangelical Christianity, professing believers increasingly know less and less of the Bible. Even graduates of leading evangelical Christian colleges are unfamiliar with the text, unschooled in its teaching. They have become adherents of the Bible by osmosis. They aren't readers, they aren't students; therefore, they aren't real disciples.

Can evangelical Christianity survive its own malnourishment? Not if the Bread of Life remains unbroken, undistributed, uneaten. Perhaps what we need most to reclaim from the Christian humanists of centuries past is their allegiance and fidelity to the Word of God as their primary source of truth.

Chapter 8

Thinking in Christian Categories

> *The purpose of a Christian education would not be merely to make men and women pious Christians: a system which aimed too rigidly at this end alone would become only obscurantist. A Christian education would primarily train people to be able to think in Christian categories.*
>
> T. S. Eliot

*T*he "first and greatest commandment" makes it plain that we're to love the Lord our God with all our mind. Since that's the main point of this book, why do we need a special chapter on this topic? Because loving God with the mind will always result in promoting the cause and purposes of genuine Christian education in all its best and most beneficial forms.

CHRISTIAN EDUCATION BELONGS EVERYWHERE

Christian education begins in the Christian home, as parents offer their children the *paideia* and *nouthesia*, the training and instruction, of the Lord. Christian education continues in the church, where worship is exemplified, where fellowship and service grow as a result of learning to adore a holy God. Christian education is needed for the workplace, where the realities of the secular and pagan culture clash with the Bible's teaching. Christian education is also tested in the state-sponsored schools and colleges, where it's increasingly under fire as the dogmas of "tolerance" and "pluralism" disallow the teaching of biblical, or even of Judeo-Christian, values.

Our homes, our churches, our businesses, our schools are the social structures in which we function as persons, as citizens of one nation or another, as representatives of the kingdom of God on earth. We need to begin to think differently about the way we live and love, the way we worship and serve, the way we work to earn our livelihood, the way we learn and teach. We need more than just novel ideas and better mousetraps; rather, we need distinctive thinking, the kind of thinking that results in distinctly different action.

To achieve such thinking, we need to understand what T. S. Eliot refers to as being "able to think in Christian categories." This means being able to define and hold to a world-and-life view oriented in Scripture; it means seeing from a Christian vantage point; it means thinking with the mind of Christ.

Thinking about Truth with a Capital T

In quite specific terms, the foundation for thinking in Christian categories is Truth with a capital T. God is truth, and all truth is of God. We need to say this again and often: *God is truth, and all truth is of God.* Whatever truth is, God is, and so, to paraphrase Justin Martyr and Augustine of Hippo and all the Christian humanists, whatever is true finds its origin in God.

God's essence is truth. Another way to speak of the character of God would be to speak in terms of absolute truth. When human beings attempt to contemplate what it means to commune with God, our most impossible thought is that we should ever attempt to deceive God, to lie to God. Conversely, it's equally impossible that God would ever lie to us.

Furthermore, God's truth is personal, not a cosmic abstraction; God's truth is historical, not merely mythic; God's truth is verbal, not incomprehensible. God's truth is known to us as the Word of God. God's truth is, first, the Word uttering the fiats of Creation and bringing into being the creatures made in love. Then comes the Word as Covenant, raising up a people out of sterile loins, a nation whose identity is indelibly marked by faith. Next, we encounter the Word as Law, God's mandate for holiness, too overwhelming in its demands for human capability. To summon men and women to a consciousness of their sin, God's Word is spoken as Prophecy through the mouth of a seer fearlessly proclaiming, "Thus saith the Lord!"

But the prophet is only God's spokesman, God's messenger. God the Father has chosen this avenue to speak to the mass of humanity through his representative—an envoy, an interlocutor, an ambassador, a voice for God. Since the Fall of Adam and Eve and their exile from Eden, the Father has cut himself off from daily, immediate communication; instead, he chooses to speak through his messengers. By Noah to his contemporaries; by Joseph to his brothers and the Egyptians; by Moses to the people of Israel; by Samuel and the other judges; by Nathan to David; by Elijah to Ahab and Jezebel; by Isaiah to Hezekiah; by Daniel to Nebuchadnezzar—as the author of the Letter to the Hebrews declares: "In the past God spoke to our forefathers through the prophets at many times and in various ways" (Hebrews 1:1).

The Truth Incarnate

But now, says the same writer, God provides another voice to speak the Word, to live the Word, to *be* the Word—the Divine Logos, the Message and the Messenger in One—the Incarnate Word, the Liberating Word, the Word-Made-Flesh in Bethlehem's stable.

This voice identifies himself as the truth because he alone knows himself to be "the image of the invisible God" (Colossians 1:15), the *eikōn*, the exact likeness of his Father, exemplifying his Father's Word. With power only truth can grant, he creates and recreates wine from water, life from death; he offers the covenant of discipleship to those who will follow and obey; he provides a law of love for God and neighbor as the only means of fulfilling the impossible old law; he prophesies the coming kingdom. Then he sums up his message of Good News in an act at once so humble and so grand as to stun the world forever: he dies, yet by his Father's Word returns to life, victorious over death.

"I am the way and the truth and the life," said Jesus of Nazareth (John 14:6). Throughout the twenty centuries since Jesus spoke those commanding words, faith has been the seal that guarantees the veracity of his claim. There's no empirical way to gauge the truthfulness of God, revealed in the One who declares himself to be the embodiment of truth; no scientific proof to offer in evidence that God was indeed in Christ to reconcile the world unto himself. The only test of God's unfailing truthfulness is the personal test of faith: Does God keep his Word?

If by faith we can answer, "Yes, I know that God is faithful," that's proof enough. Our faith becomes a key that unlocks the treasure chest of God's promises. Until we can answer with such assurance—until we're ready to acknowledge who God is and his sovereign right to make the rules by which we play the game—we'll never know the reality of truth in any sphere.

In human dealings, we're quite accustomed to broken vows and shattered pledges. Part of growing out of childhood's naiveté and into adult responsibility is learning to cope with life's broken promises. If we're at all sophisticated shoppers, we read the fine print before putting our money down; we wait for the obligatory disclaimer explaining away all the advertising's sweet-talk. We've all been burned too many times!

Sometimes we're the victims, sometimes the perpetrators. "But, Daddy," a disappointed child accuses, "you *promised!*" So, to protect ourselves against being held too closely to our word, we learn to hedge our promises with qualifiers; conditional phrases become our escape hatch. Our "yes" means "maybe yes, maybe no." It's called the fine art of equivocation, and we use it all the time.

CHRISTIAN EDUCATION TEACHES THE CHARACTER OF GOD

But God doesn't engage in equivocation. His "yes" means simply that. St. Paul told the Corinthians,

> For the Son of God, Jesus Christ, who was preached among you by me and Silas and Timothy, was not "Yes" and "No," but in him it has always been "Yes." For no matter how many promises God has made, they are "Yes" in Christ (2 Corinthians 1:19-20).

God backs his Word by his absolute holiness of character. He simply can't lie, can't fail to keep his promise. God can be depended on to keep his Word. But to guarantee his promise, God offers the gift of the Holy Spirit to be our *paraclete*, our constant Companion and Comforter. So St. Paul continues,

> Now it is God who makes both us and you stand firm in Christ. He anointed us, set his seal of ownership on us, and put his Spirit in our hearts as a deposit, guaranteeing what is to come (2 Corinthians 1:21- 22).

As the presence of the Spirit within us becomes evident, our lives become microcosms of God's intention for every human being. We experience a re-creation; we share in a new covenant of grace; we learn to live by the law of love; we find ourselves able and willing to declare the word of the Lord—all by faith in God's faithfulness.

So to think in Christian categories means, first, to think about "whatever is true" (Philippians 4:8). When we do, the rest will follow: "whatever is noble . . . right . . . pure . . . lovely . . . admirable—if anything is excellent or praiseworthy, think about such things."

Integrating Truth and Life

But to think about truth, to contemplate truth, to recognize truth, to seek out the truth is no easy task. It requires a perspective on reality derived from wholeness—an integrated perspective. In Christian academic circles, particularly in evangelical and reformed environments, a phrase has been circulating for some time. Professors and students on those campuses have become accustomed to hearing annual pep-talks on their need to achieve an "integration of faith and learning," blending as one their expression of Christian faith and their studies of the arts and sciences.

This is a noble goal, but integration should not be limited to faith and learning; it must reach beyond the realm of formal education. Christians who desire to think about truth can't pick and choose when it suits them to adopt an integrated mind-set. Instead, we need to strive for wholeness in every phase of our lives; we need to work toward an integration of faith and *living*.

For some reason, American politicians have severe problems understanding this necessity. A discredited philanderer, one of whose victims drowned in a tidal pond while he strove to disguise his part in her death, seems to have no difficulty in pontificating about someone else's threat to women's rights! A discredited plagiarist, who professes not to have known that quoting without proper attribution is called cheating, withdraws from the presidential campaign but finds no reason to discontinue his duties as a United States senator and chairman of the Judiciary Committee! A congressman whose admitted homosexual partners in perversion include the young boys serving as pages is nonetheless free to intone his views on human rights in Central America! These men, mere examples, have no apparent concept of wholeness of character; their constituents require nothing of the sort.

Why not? Because most of us likewise live utterly fragmented lives ourselves. For a long time, the morality of our society has cloaked itself in a "Sunday-go-to-meetin' " mentality. Like clockwork, we know how to appear pious for an hour or so once a week, on Sunday morning. The rest of the week, we may choose to divest ourselves of almost any semblance of godliness at home, school, or business. No wonder pollsters record that the leading cause of unbelief among the unchurched, year after year, is "hypocrisy," the phoniness of a professed faith that has no substance in weekday and workplace experience.

Truth as Knowledge

If we mean anything at all by our claim to believe that God is Truth, that Jesus Christ is Truth, that the Spirit is Truth, that God's Word is Truth, then we need to think and live in truth. To help us think in truth, let's remember that God himself is interested in conveying truth through human knowledge. God is no respecter of persons: He doesn't prefer a genius over a mental incompetent; he loves both equally. But God rejoices as a thinking person struggles to resolve a problem. God laughs with pleasure as a student works her way through a difficult lesson, as a teacher enables his class to glimpse a facet of truth, as a researcher explores a new territory of truth, as an artist perceives a new vision of truth.

Furthermore, we human beings have a direct responsibility to God our Creator, first, to learn whatever can be known, then to teach that knowledge to others. Of course, as Christians we believe that we have a primary obligation to teach the truth of the gospel, to go into all the world and make disciples, as the Great Commission of our Lord demands. But our obligation to share truth with others goes beyond the limits of truth about salvation; it also includes a different sort of truth,

truth whose purpose is to help mankind fulfill the mandate given in Eden, to be the guardians and propagators of both nature and human nature, the human race and its cultures.

Therefore, we must impart truth in all its manifestations: truth about health and hygiene, truth about water pollution and the ozone layer, truth about the hazards of cigarette smoking, truth about the dangers and benefits inherent in nuclear power, truth about the joy of sexual relations in marriage and the emptiness of promiscuity, truth about the virtues of parental responsibility and the wretched consequences of aimlessness, truth about the inestimable treasure of knowledge and the blight of ignorance.

Truth as Wisdom

Another way of saying the same thing is to speak in biblical terms of *wisdom* and *knowledge*. What we must learn and teach about God's sovereignty, Jesus Christ's incarnation and atonement, his death and resurrection, his expected return, the work of the Holy Spirit through the Word and through the Church—all these are in the realm of God's *wisdom*. Its content lies in God's province, to be known and understood only by faith; God's mystery, wiser in its apparent foolishness than all of human reason. Not to know and believe God's *wisdom* makes fools of human creatures, no matter how brilliant our intellects.

But we who claim by faith to possess God's wisdom must also learn and teach human *knowledge*—the arts and sciences, the practical skills and common sense, the powers of observation and inference, the data bank of memory and retention—for to the best of our human abilities, such knowledge can also be a means of leading us to an understanding of truth. For God is not only the author of *wisdom* but also the author of *knowledge*. God is the original Teacher, mankind the original pupil. Therefore God is involved in the discovery and transmission of all we come to know, retain, and pass on to others. When we read and ponder, when we experiment and learn, when we think and extrapolate and project and thereafter *know*, God is the source of that knowledge.

A Curious Problem: When Error Poses as Truth

This raises a curious problem: If God is a participant in our struggle to attain human knowledge, why do we sometimes elevate to the place of authentic truth that which is only a distortion of truth or even the opposite of truth? Why do we insist for centuries that the earth is flat or that the earth is the center of the universe or that some other race has been cursed by God with a skin color different from ours or that the Creation occurred only six thousand years ago on a Tuesday?

One answer to this puzzle may be our eagerness to pinpoint ready solutions to complex problems; another answer may be our simplemindedness in assuming that the conventional wisdom of earlier generations needs no reexamining; another, our facile assumption that what appears on the surface must be reality; still another, our fear of facing up to the consequences of a changed or changing perception of truth, which leads to the final and most deadening reason of all: the conviction that all truth as human knowledge has already been made known and that to question its validity or search for alternatives is heresy.

Instead of fear in the face of human knowledge, we need faith, humility, and forthrightness. We need to affirm, first, our faith that whatever may become known in the future is already known to an omniscient God and will ultimately reveal his greater glory. Second, we need the grace to admit our own insufficiency as thinkers. The fact is, we don't "know it all" about anything! The words of Oliver Cromwell to the General Assembly of the Church of Scotland—concerning the Scots' claim that Charles II was their lawful king—apply to us in many circumstances: "I beseech you, in the bowels of Christ, think it possible you may be mistaken." How often we've needed just such a deflating of our error-ridden dogma! How rare to find someone who summons us to a reconsidered opinion "in the bowels of Christ"—this quaint seventeenth-century phrase, based on a correlation of the emotions with the various organs of the body, is translated by the NIV as "the affection of Christ Jesus" (Philippians 1:8).

Third, we need courage to persevere in the quest for knowledge wherever it leads, certain that God himself desires to have us know all that can and remains to be known about his Creation and our part in it. We may not succeed in learning more than a nugget of whatever vast knowledge is yet to be mined, but our calling as human beings blessed with the divine attribute of reason compels the expedition forward.

God the Father's Delight in Understanding

We can confidently assert that God is interested in human knowledge and in our coming to grasp it ourselves. Just as a parent eagerly watches a toddler learning how to speak and walk and handle objects, God the Father delights as we become more and more acquainted with and informed about the universe given to us to enjoy. And with the certainty of God's interest and involvement in human knowledge, we can also assert our moral responsibility to meet God at the intersection of wisdom and knowledge, which is *understanding*—a spiritual gift which empowers us, like Solomon, with differentiation, discernment, and discrimination.

We're granted the capacity to recognize the difference between facts and opinions; we're called upon to practice discernment as we infer and develop our own principles of truth; we're expected to discriminate between evidences of truth and evidences of falsehood. All the while, we're also summoned to exercise the faculty called *imagination*, whose root is simple childlike curiosity about everything in God's world.

Furthermore, the search for knowledge is no fanciful amusement or entertainment for our idleness. It's a requirement of our stewardship as human beings made for the praise of God. Charles Malik, whom I've quoted in an earlier chapter, speaks strongly to this point in his book, *A Christian Critique of the University*. Malik fearlessly asks an almost scandalous question, "What does Jesus Christ think of the university?" He isn't concerned primarily with what the university thinks of Jesus Christ, although the modern university's deliberate choice to ignore and treat with contempt the Lord Jesus Christ pained Malik. Still Malik insisted on his question and its answer.

> The question, What does Jesus Christ think of the university? is valid, and it has an answer. We may not know the answer, but the answer *exists*, and we may expectantly seek it; if it eludes us, it is still there.

Malik continued,

> Since the university determines the course of events and the destiny of man more than any other institution or agency today, it is impossible for a Christian not to ask the question: What does Jesus Christ think of the university? To a Christian this question is an absolute imperative.

ASKING THE POINTED QUESTION: WHAT DOES JESUS THINK?

So too the same question may be asked as it applies to every human institution and activity, every element and particle of nature. As the creating and sustaining Lord of the universe, what does Jesus Christ think of the San Andreas fault and the likelihood of its producing an earthquake of devastating proportions to the millions of human beings who have chosen to live their lives along its fissure? What does Jesus Christ think about mankind's attempts to come to terms with nuclear energy, both for peaceful uses and for belligerent or deterrent uses? What does Jesus Christ think about political systems, economic theories, or architectural styles? What does

Jesus Christ think of the latest innovation in human fertility? What does Jesus Christ think of the Olympic Games?

Thinking about Home, Church, Work, and School

But on a far more personal level, we must also ask: What does Jesus Christ think of my relationship with my spouse? with our children? with my in-laws? with other members of my family? What does Jesus Christ think of our family budget? the last major purchase we made? the vacation trip we're planning? the retirement home we're considering? Does it matter to Jesus Christ whether I jog or walk, play golf or tennis? Does Jesus Christ wish me to know the truth about my domestic life?

What does Jesus Christ think of my worship and service through the church we attend? the Christian missions and other philanthropic agencies we support? Does it matter to Jesus Christ that, after years of active leadership in independent churches, our present church is hierarchical, our family's worship is now formal and liturgical rather than casual and spontaneous? Is there yet more truth that Jesus Christ wishes me to know about the Church and my worship?

What does Jesus Christ think of my job, the means by which I earn my livelihood? What does Jesus Christ think of my work on that job, my faithfulness as an employee or employer? What does Jesus Christ think of the course my professional career has taken? What does Jesus Christ think of my earning power in one position as against another? Does it matter to Jesus Christ that I've chosen to remain in one setting for more than thirty years when other opportunities invited relocation? Does it matter to Jesus Christ that my wife is a union member and I'm not? Is there still more truth to be learned about my vocation?

What does Jesus Christ think of the books I read, the music I listen to, the television programs and movies I watch, the professional self-improvement courses I take, the entertainment I enjoy? What does Jesus Christ think of how I vote? the magazines we subscribe to, the videotapes of old movies we rent, the restaurants and theaters that now interest us? Does it matter to Jesus Christ whether, in all my lifetime, I've ever had a seemingly original thought or always relied on the thinking of others? or that, as we mature, our tastes have changed and enlarged? Is there other truth about my lifelong learning that Jesus Christ would have me know?

And what does Jesus Christ think of the education our children receive at home, at church, at school? What does Jesus Christ think of our choice to enroll our children in the local public school? Or what does Jesus Christ think of our insistence that our children attend a Christian school or be taught by us at home?

An Admittedly Biased Opinion

Perhaps it won't surprise you to hear from someone who's spent more than thirty years in a school whose entire board, administration, and faculty unitedly acknowledge the Lordship of Jesus Christ—a school where the Bible is taught as the authoritative Word of God, a school where God is regarded as the Source of all truth; in other words, a *Christian school*— perhaps it won't surprise you to hear me say that Christian education can be nurtured in such an environment.

But let's not mistake the Christian school for anything other than a *school*. It's not an incubator from the temptations of the world, the flesh, and the devil. The Christian school is also not a penal institution for the incarceration of wayward sons and daughters from Christian homes. As long as there are human beings involved, every Christian school will have its share of human iniquity. The difference is that in such a school, girls and boys will learn the power of redemption, the cleansing of forgiveness, the strength of prayer, the promises of Scripture. The Christian school is a training ground, a place of elementary and secondary instruction in the rudiments of loving God with all the mind, strength, soul, and heart.

To sum up, the primary and only legitimate reason for the existence of a Christian school is to be a place of academic teaching and learning, where girls and boys are nurtured by the example of their teachers to become followers of Jesus Christ, thinking and acting like his disciples, enjoying to the full all of God's gifts of grace.

OBEDIENT ACTION FOLLOWS THE ANSWER

So, to have our minds renewed to resemble the mind of Christ, we need to be asking ourselves these kinds of questions: What does Jesus Christ think of the most elemental aspect of our daily lives? How is that truth made apparent to us? For evangelical Christians the confirmation of truth will always be found in the Scripture's confirming promise—not some proof text taken out of proper setting, but part of the whole counsel of God. So to know what Jesus Christ thinks about any issue, we need to know what corresponding precept or truth-principle the Bible teaches.

But then follows the next question: How is my action determined by what Jesus Christ thinks, by what the Bible teaches? For all our thinking must be accompanied by action—thinking and acting like a Christian.

In 1896, a Congregationalist pastor named Charles M. Sheldon wrote a book called *In His Steps*. Sheldon believed that the Sermon on the Mount should be applied to everyday life. His book asked a straightforward question: "What would Jesus do?"

To begin thinking *and* acting like Jesus Christ, we need to ask that same question. Its answers may astonish us.

PART THREE

TRANSFORMED LIVES

Chapter 9

Worthy Words

> *As every writer worth his salt very well knows, there is only one specific, irreplaceable term that fits into a certain situation. It is the knack of hitting upon such terms continually, often by dint of laborious effort, which distinguishes the great stylist and helps dress the truth in beautiful garb.*
> Emile Cailliet

*M*ost of us enjoy a good conversation, a stimulating dialogue with an informed and witty speaker. The give-and-take of conflicting opinions, the flash of insight, the intensity of keenly honed argument—all these can be found in exhilarating conversation. But the word *conversation* has a broader meaning than mere talk. It comes from the Latin verb *conversari*, meaning "to live with, to keep company with." Its archaic, now obsolete, usage denotes behavior and conduct, one's manner of life.

The word occurs some twenty times in the King James Version, as in Philippians 1:27, "Only let your conversation be as it becometh the gospel of Christ." Here the Apostle Paul is calling upon the Christians in Philippi—as the NIV states—to "conduct yourselves in a manner worthy of the gospel of Christ."

We all have choices to make in respect to our behavior. Christians and pagans, believers and atheists, evangelicals and secularists—we all must make a new choice almost every minute we breathe. For the most part these choices are tiny decisions; some of them ethical choices (Do I support animal rights or do I buy my wife a fur coat?); others amoral decisions (Shall I put butter or margarine on my toast?); only a few truly moral matters (How can I honestly decline an invitation, without lying, when I have no real reason not to accept?).

But each of these decisions accumulates into a mode of conduct, a behavior that constitutes my "conversation," my manner of living. St. Paul suggests that Christians may choose either to adorn or debase the gospel by our conduct. So for each of us, the question becomes plain: Does my "conversation" complement the gospel I profess to believe? Is my manner of life, my conduct, congruent with what I claim to be true—that I'm a redeemed child of God, different from what I might be, transformed through faith in Jesus Christ? Or is my behavior unworthy of the gospel of Christ?

THE SIGNIFICANCE OF WORDS

A causal relationship exists between thought and conduct. The way we behave is a consequence of how we think, what we value, the priorities we establish. But there's also a *bridge* between thought and action. That bridge is speech, the words we speak, the way we talk and write. Nothing tells more about our thinking process than the words we utter measured by the acts we commit. Our most memorable speeches—for instance, Lincoln's Gettysburg Address—are examples of careful, thoughtful construction, those parallel phrases indicating the seriousness of the matter. But our most spontaneous and blurted remarks are also a reflection of what we really think, the world-and-life view that both shapes and describes our comprehension of reality.

That's why it's imperative that every Christian, wishing to think and act like Jesus Christ, become more and more aware of language because we are people of the Word. Our God has chosen to reveal himself as a *speaking* God, a *writing* God, a *communicating* God. He speaks the fiats of Creation; he inscribes the Ten Commandments in stone; he communicates directly through his Spirit and his Word, indirectly through history and nature. When he chooses to reveal himself in person, it is as the Word-made-flesh that he appears in the guise of an Aramaic-speaking man. When that Incarnation has served its eternal purposes in redemption, God chooses to offer us a lasting written record, inspired by the authority of his Spirit.

It's wholly orthodox to say that all we know of God, all we have to hold onto—our faith in Jesus Christ, our guidance by the Holy Spirit, our encouragement from Scripture—all we can claim is *words*. God's grace makes these words real; they become life and hope to us. But they are words nonetheless. As such, we need to treasure and preserve the gift of language; we need to elevate the significance of language and protect it from tarnished misuse.

May I illustrate with a personal experience? Some years ago I was invited to give a convocation address at a college in New England. A few weeks earlier, blood vessels in my left eye had hemorrhaged, leaving me totally blind in that eye. I told anyone who asked, "I've had an accident with my eye." Many kind people offered to pray for me, but no one corrected my use of language, and so I went on talking about my accidental loss of vision.

The night before I was to speak, I flew from New York to Providence. The weather was foul. When the plane landed, I sat looking out at the mist rolling in off Narragansett Bay. Through that murk I saw eventually the illuminated sign identifying the airport. One word seemed to pulsate through the fog, like a neon sign going on and off then on again. PROVIDENCE ... PROVIDENCE ... PROVIDENCE. I'm a Baptist preacher's son, and I've studied some theology, but never before that night had I ever thought through the meaning of the doctrine of providence.

Ruefully, I realized that I'd been guilty of something far worse than the mere casual, unthinking misuse of language. I'd carelessly demeaned the Lord of the universe, *Jehovah-jireh*, the God who provides. By telling friends of my "accident," I'd been saying, in effect, "I live by chance in a world that is no more than a vast cosmic casino. I live by the random rules of accident in a world governed by happenstance and chaos."

Trusting God means delivering over to him responsibility for all that lies beyond my power to control. Providence doesn't mean that Christians never have an automobile collision; it means that Christians never have an *accident*. Providence means that when Christians encounter an incident of disappointment or even death, the God we serve provides the fortitude we need to see us through the difficulties of our lives. This is what St. Paul assures the Corinthians:

> None of the trials which have come upon you is more than a human being can stand. You can trust that God will not let you be put to the test beyond your strength, but with any trial will also provide a way out by enabling you to put up with it (1 Corinthians 10:13, The New Jerusalem Bible).

For such a God, the word "accident" isn't in his vocabulary—or as I heard a broadcaster on a Los Angeles station put it, "Our God never has to say 'Oops!'"

Language is an important monitor. Thoughtful speech, the careful choice of words, is one of the marks of maturity, spiritual as well as chronological. What we say and how we say it matters because what we say and how we say it is a direct reflection of who we are—or who we pretend to be! Jesus himself made the connection: "For out of the overflow of the heart the mouth speaks" (Matthew 12:34). From the deepest recesses of our being comes the dead giveaway: the words we say. So no thinking Christian can speak of *luck*, good or bad *fortune*, *chance*, or *coincidence* because, like "accident," these too are words foreign to faith in the God-who-provides.

Spokesmen for God

Thought and speech are inextricable from behavior. If we're to think and act like Christ, we must also become conscious that our words are signs and labels; they identify the speaker and the speaker's world-and-life view. They tell more about the speaker than many of us realize. Is our speech appropriate to our calling as God's envoys? Only if we think and act as those who have accepted God's commission to be spokesmen on his behalf. The prophet Jeremiah records that commission as he heard it:

> "If you repent, I will restore you
>   that you may serve me;
> if you utter worthy, not worthless, words,
>   you will be my spokesman" (Jeremiah 15:19).

Not that God necessarily needs you and me. If he chooses, God can speak from a burning bush or even through the braying of a donkey. God is also perfectly capable of speaking directly, unmistakably, terrifyingly, as on the walls of Belshazzar's palace. Furthermore, God will speak again with the voice of a trumpet on the day of history's consummation. To the dead, he will say, "Rise up!" To the living, "Come, for all things are now ready."

But for now, God chooses to speak through us, his human messengers. He speaks and acts through human agents. God whispers his will in the ear of the one who listens and obeys. He calls by name, "Samuel, Samuel," to which the only appropriate reply is, "Speak, for your servant is listening." He calls for volunteers: "Whom shall I send? And who will go for us?" To this challenge the only proper response is, "Here am I. Send me."

No, God doesn't need us; he has angels to do his bidding. But because God is pleased to share responsibility for this planet and this race's wellbeing with us, the creatures made in his own image, God commissions willing ambassadors to speak the message of truth, the word of warning, the word of comfort, the word of hope, the word of joy.

Conditions for Service

But God's commission carries with it a set of conditions, qualifications we must meet before we can become his messengers. God imposes careful standards upon those who would be his spokesmen. *If* we meet his criteria, *then* our work will be effective; if we fail to measure up, our work will be useless.

Some of us seem to possess a peculiarly exalted notion of our own importance to the work of God. We act as though Almighty God were so weak and dependent upon us, the kingdom would collapse without us to hold it up. We are indispensable—or so we suppose—and the need God has is so critical, the emergency so acute, that God will accept any service we offer on our own terms. In arrogance we present ourselves, like impure vessels, not realizing that God abhors our sin. We present ourselves as leaky vases, presuming to contain the splendor of God's grace. We present ourselves as damaged goods, remnants from a fire sale, and expect to model the righteousness of God.

Too often we ignore God's conditions for service, which are, bluntly put, *If/then*; *if not/then no way*! We go on assuming that the warnings of Jesus Christ apply to somebody else less well connected with the evangelical subculture—somebody, perhaps, who never heard of the Four Spiritual Laws or the Urbana Conference. But not to us! Not to us will the Lord we have claimed to represent turn and say, "I never knew you!" Yet isn't that precisely the warning to anyone daring to slight God's stated conditions for accepting God's commission?

Worthy Words

And what conditions does God impose? God evaluates the content of our message: "If you utter worthy, not worthless, words, you will be my spokesman." What constitutes "worthless words"? If we're intent on thinking and acting like Christians, it's surely fitting to assert that style and content, form and message, are indivisible. So once again, we must cry out against careless, imprecise, sloppy speech—often a reflection of careless, imprecise, and sloppy thinking—as a supposedly satisfactory vehicle for communicating the Good News. I like what Elton Trueblood has said:

> We must, as Christians, stress excellence. Holy shoddy is still shoddy. . . . You have some reason to doubt the religious experience of a student who murders the English language. It ought to be part of the Christian religion to know the difference between the nominative and objective cases.

Furthermore, much of our God-talk, when not ungrammatical or malaprop, is often threadbare from casual, automatic, tongue-twitching overuse. A writer in *Harper's* picks up some of the flavor of current evangelical-ese, featuring

> familiar words used in slightly unfamiliar ways—words like burden, fellowship, and shared. Thus, in the evangelical jargon, you never wanted to send some Bibles to the Indians, but "had a burden for the Indians," and you never just plain got together with other Christians, but "fellowshipped" with them, and you never flat-out told anybody anything, but "shared," as in "Floyd shared what Jesus did for his hemorrhoids."

Can we learn from this gibe at our evangelical language—its often mindless repetitiousness, its patterns of predictable utterance, the constant gibberish of our particular evangelical clubhouse? Or are we looking to excuse ourselves by exclaiming, "Why does it matter how we speak and what we say? What difference does it make, just so the general idea about the gospel gets through?" What difference indeed! What difference if we say *infer* when we mean *imply*? or *uninterested* when we mean *disinterested*? Let's remember that Scripture doesn't suggest that "In the beginning was the General Idea"; nor does the Bible record that, at the Incarnation, "the Vague Notion became flesh and dwelt among us."

We can never grow tired of asserting that Jesus of Nazareth is the definitive Logos, Divine Logic, Sublime Reason, the Alpha and Omega, the Everlasting Yes. Our best attempts at articulating this mystery will always fall short of full expression, but that gives us no right to absolve ourselves for selling out to the cheap phrase, the easy cliche.

Worthless Words

Worthless words are also sanctimonious sentiments without Scriptural foundation. We hear this all too often in the lyrics of contemporary music reputedly Christian—earnestness gone awry, devotion without discretion, and most appallingly, a failure to recognize the synthesis between form and content. But even more distressing is the refusal of some contemporary Christian musicians to conform to biblical standards of Christian morality. Their words are worthless until confession and restitution have been made; thereafter, they may be restored to service less flamboyant, more humble, more in keeping with the modesty becoming to servants of Jesus Christ.

But professional musicians aren't alone in their oblivious absorption in the cesspools of popular culture. Perhaps the most lethal, the most overtly satanic aspect of recent popular culture has been the music of death played and sung by devotees of so- called "heavy metal" rock music. Still, many professing Christians not only ignore the dangers of this noxious music but seem to revel in its blasphemy.

I remember well a moment of insight given me by a student at an evangelical college in the Midwest. I was sitting in the student union with an older freshman, a man of twenty-five years but looking more than fifty—scant of hair and teeth, his face marred, his arms gouged by years of drug addiction. It was November. The previous summer, on a street in Los Angeles, he'd been handed a flyer announcing an evangelistic meeting nearby. There he'd heard the gospel for the first time. The next day, momentarily clear of his usual drugged state, he'd returned to the church and professed faith in Christ. The pastor saw something in this man and prevailed upon his own college to take the new convert into summer school, even though the man had dropped out of junior high school, already an addict by age fourteen.

The college had taken him; he'd survived summer school and been admitted to conditional freshman standing. Struggling with both the demands of college and his newly redeemed life, what puzzled him most was the inconsistency of the Christians around him. As we talked, he paused for a moment to hear the music being piped throughout the lounge from the main desk of the student union, one of the then-current Top Forty.

This young Christian, with his battered face and rotten teeth—yet radiating joy in Christ—said to me, "They shouldn't oughta play that music here. These people here, they don't know what it means. They've never been on the other side of the door. But me, I've been on the other side of the door, and Mister, it means death!"

If we are to think, speak, and act like Christians, we should be committed to life, not death. Our conversation—our manner of living—must transcend the best that the secular culture has to offer with the best that the Lord of heaven and earth has to give: abundant life, life with a purpose fulfilling itself day by day.

But just as culpable as popular musicians in uttering worthless words are many radio and television preachers—and their equally tawdry wives. Until the rash of scandals in religious broadcasting that surfaced in 1987 and 1988, some of these televangelists, whose pulpit is the Church of the Unholy Trinitron, seemed almost immune from judgment. Then came the series of outrageous events all too well known to every Christian. How worthless now seem the pious words of sexual perverts and their greed-driven wives.

And there, but for the grace of God, go I.

Enough of celebrity-bashing. The secular media have already told us more than we wish to know about these wretched reminders that sin is real—as if any of us needed such reminders! In these lurid headlines we can find no cause for self-satisfaction. Rather we need to caution each other with the warning words of St. Paul, "So, if you think you are standing firm, be careful that you don't fall!" (1 Corinthians 10:12).

Conversation that Adorns the Gospel

We also need to ask ourselves this pointed question: Is my life any different from that of my law-abiding, tax-paying, but essentially godless neighbor? Does my speech commend to him a life transformed and transforming by the power of the blood of Jesus Christ? Living next door to me or working in an adjoining office, do my acquaintances recognize in me any quality of thought, speech, or action that represents Jesus Christ to them? Am I as eager to talk about eternal verities as I am to show photos of our darling grandchildren or describe my latest accomplishment on the golf course? Do I, in fact, comprehend the difference between worthy and worthless words?

What about worthy words? Language consistent with new life in Christ, lived under his Lordship. Language that speaks of faith, hope, love, and gives thanks; language that acknowledges God's providence and gives praise; language bathed in the precepts of Scripture; language fresh with one's own experience as a bearer of the Good News; language that

points away from oneself as messenger, pointing instead to the
message of life, light, and liberty. Worthy words spring to
reality in a life transformed by renewed thinking about what it
means to be redeemed by the Cross; a transformed life marked
by acts of grace and humility.

Chapter 10

Reciprocal Love

The way we treat others is the way we treat God.

Peter K. Haile

Now we come to the nub of the issue. It's all fine and dandy to issue pronouncements about such esoteric subjects as thinking with the mind of Christ, to make declarations about the power of language and other semi-abstractions; it's quite another matter to begin dealing with practical issues of living out the reality of Christ's life in us. But that's the point at which we've finally arrived, and there's no turning back.

What should be the common denominator in acting like a Christian? How should we be expected to live according to the faith we profess?

THE MARK OF LOVE

From the earliest years of the Christian era, one characteristic has marked those whose lives have been transformed by the Cross. Jesus Christ himself both commended and commanded that the sign of faithful disciples be their reciprocal love.

> A new command I give you: *Love one another*. As I have loved you, so you must *love one another*. By this all men will know that you are my disciples, if you *love one another* (John 13:34-35, italics mine).

> My command is this: *Love each other* as I have loved you. Greater love has no one than this, that he lay down his life for his friends. You are my friends if you do what I command. . . . This is my command: *Love each other* (John 15:12-14, 17, italics mine).

Reciprocal love—the love or *agape* prescribed by Jesus of Nazareth—is our primary mark of submission to the Lordship of Jesus Christ. Such love means mutual esteem, mutual regard, an exchange of concern, a transfer of delight from what pleases me alone to what pleases others. *Agape* removes the focus from self and turns its concentration upon others.

The Testimony of the Early Church

How well did the first Christians exemplify this sign of reciprocal love? We know certainly that their number included frauds like Ananias and Sapphira. St. Paul tells us of others who failed the test: deserters like Demas, Phygelus, and Hermogenes; blasphemers such as Hymenaeus and Alexander; troublemakers like Euodia and Syntyche. We also know that, even among the apostles themselves, disputes between Peter and Paul or Paul and Barnabas divided the effort to evangelize the world. No, the first Christians weren't entirely free from pride, envy, or self-interest.

But we must remember other names as well: Priscilla and Aquila, who "risked their lives" for Paul; the household of Stephanas, who "devoted themselves to the service of the saints"; Onesiphorus, who was not ashamed of Paul's imprisonment and searched the Roman prisons until he found him; a fellow-prisoner named Aristarchus; a runaway slave called Onesimus and his master Philemon, who received him back into his household; others such as Timothy, Luke, Tychicus, and Epaphroditus, of whose compassion and acts of kindness the Apostle speaks in his letters.

The testimony of the early church goes well beyond its own community. One ancient writer, commenting on the new religious phenomenon emerging from the Roman-occupied territory called Palestine, spoke of the Christians he had seen in the arena, mismatched against ravenous lions. Something in their behavior toward their fellows touched him, and he wrote, "Behold, how they love each other!"

Love for Others

Reciprocal love! The surest indication that Christians have begun to experience what it means to love the Lord God with heart, soul, strength, and mind isn't a passing grade on some test of super-piety, like walking on live coals or casting out demons. There's no such thing as "victorious Christian living" or "the deeper life" or any of the other pat descriptions of so-called spiritual maturity apart from an active, demonstrable love between Christians. The only indelible mark of authentic love for God is a divinely aroused compassion for the needs of others. Loving God in all four dimensions of our being begins with the social and emotional dimension, the heart. Its practical application comes through loving our neighbor as ourselves.

Show me a professing Christian whose heart is dull to the needs of others—whose jokes are frequently at the expense of ethnic minorities, whose respect for the opposite sex is minimal, whose compassion for the less gifted or less privileged seems stillborn—and I'll show you someone whose religion suffers from arrested development and stunted growth.

Love Within Families

Furthermore, loving God by loving others begins with our nearest "neighbors," the members of our own household, our own family. Have you ever noticed how rapidly a mean and nasty tone of voice during a domestic quarrel changes when the telephone rings? We may be in the middle of a shouting match at each other, but when the telephone is answered, the decibels drop to a purring "Hello?" We may be launching salvos of snide remarks and sarcastic innuendo, but as soon as the phone rings, our tone returns to something appropriate to civilized discourse. I wonder why.

Isn't it because we take for granted our right to be more insulting to someone we profess to love than we'd ever dare to be with a stranger? Isn't it because we presume upon our familial relationship and expect our so-called "loved ones" to understand and accept our boorishness, however demeaning to them? What gives us such an exalted notion of our privileges over other family members?

Acting like a Christian begins in the family with reciprocal love and gratitude, respect and honor across the generations— between grandparents and parents, between parents and their children, between siblings, among cousins and in-laws; most of all, between husband and wife.

Marriage is a sacrament, not in the commonly misunderstood sense that any sacrament has soul-saving efficacy—only faith in the redeeming work of Jesus Christ saves—but as an outward and visible sign of an inward and invisible grace. That's what a sacrament is: a sign of holy significance. Just as wedding rings signify a whole and unbroken union between those who exchange and wear them, so the marriage union itself "signifies to us the mystery of the union between Christ and his church," as the traditional marriage service reminds us.

Have you read that marriage service recently? Have you looked again at what spouses promise each other? Have you listened carefully during the wedding ceremonies you've attended? The language may be overly familiar—"Dearly beloved, we have come together in the presence of God to witness and bless the joining together of this man and this woman in Holy Matrimony"—and so we may need to set aside a time to reread and renew our vows. For some years, my wife Lory and I have been doing this on our wedding anniversary, each December 15.

That first December 15, 1956, was a long time ago. We were both young and dazzled by the wedding event itself. Did we even consciously hear the officiating minister—my father—as he led us through the recitation of our vows? Did we have any way of understanding their true depth of meaning? "Bond and covenant of marriage"? "Love, comfort, honor, and keep?"

> For better for worse, for richer for poorer, in sickness and in health, to love and to cherish, until we are parted by death. This is my solemn vow.

The vow doesn't read "For better or for worse." It doesn't suggest two contrasting possibilities; the vow specifies one common experience consisting of both conditions: better *and* worse, richer *and* poorer, sickness *and* health. Furthermore, "to love" means "to cherish," to treasure above everyone and everything else.

Until we are parted by death.

Until we are parted by death.

UNTIL WE ARE PARTED BY DEATH.

This is the biblical ideal. If human marriage signifies the union between Christ and his church—if the Marriage Supper of the Lamb intimates the beginning of the Eternal Honeymoon—then what else can divorce represent but the crumbling of the heavenly promise? Is this why the Bridegroom loved the Bride and gave his life for her, only later to break faith with her or her with him? Or does the profound mystery of Christ and his church no longer pertain to human marriages?

The greatest gift a father can give his children is to love and cherish their mother to the end of his life. Conversely, one of the most damaging decisions parents can make is to disrupt their children's lives and security by aborting their marriage vows and disbanding the family. Over more than thirty years of working with teenagers, most of whom have come to The Stony Brook School from evangelical Christian homes, I can affirm with authority what everyone who works with youth will tell you: The most disruptive children, the most alienated and antagonistic teenagers, are those going through or surviving the aftermath of a divorce, especially the break-up of a Christian home.

A virus of selfish priorities leading to the destruction of marriages now infects the evangelical subculture with ravaging ferocity. While the national divorce rate seems to be steady, divorce among evangelicals—for whom it represents removal of the most recent taboo—seems to be accelerating. The single most distressing characteristic of contemporary evangelical Christianity is our sinful neglect of biblical standards for loving and cherishing one's own husband or wife.

Unthinkable in positions of leadership just a score of years ago, divorced persons today may be senior pastors or head their own marriage counseling bureaus with little if any sense of awkwardness. Whereas St. Paul instructed Timothy and Titus that elders and other church leaders should be "the husband of but one wife" (1 Timothy 3:12, Titus 1:6), we seem to know better. As someone has said of our society, we favor sequential rather than simultaneous bigamy. We've discovered that there are several acceptable grounds for divorce today; we've broadened from the outdated and narrow biblical stipulations to whatever a matrimonial attorney can claim in court.

I confess that my generation, come to maturity following the Korean War, must look with shame at the havoc we've brought upon the Christian family. We've permitted laxity to creep into our understanding of family obligations, a shoulder-shrugging neutrality toward marriage vows, an abdication of authority with regard to the bringing up of our children. In many respects we've failed to give our own children a model to emulate. Instead, we've sent them out into a confusing world, a society which fosters the self-centered ideal, which favors the institutionalizing of the elderly, which promotes live-in fornication rather than life-long marriage, which tosses off the blame for unruly children upon the rest of society, instead of accepting our God-ordained role as members of a Christian family.

For all this, my generation is at fault for not having had sufficient courage to oppose the incursion of decadence into our own homes. What will redeem from folly an evangelical Christian subculture not far removed from having the shameful word "Ichabod" inscribed as our motto: "The glory of the Lord has departed"? How can we break the world's despairing pattern of fractured marriages and multiple remarriages? How can we spare our children the grief of ruptured families? Only if once more we hear and heed our Lord's new commandment: "Love one another."

But what about those families in which the home is broken in every respect except by legal separation and divorce decree? Homes in which wife and husband are barely civil, homes in which the children are accustomed to an atmosphere of fury, even violence? Homes where the marriage is maintained in name only, until the day when—the last child having grown—the parents can release themselves from miserable bondage to each other? Isn't their divorce a better alternative than hypocrisy? Isn't it kinder and more Christian to free themselves and their unhappy spouse from slavery to convention?

Perhaps so. But only if you hold that God's grace is insufficient; that God's arm is shortened so that he can no longer rescue those in peril of preempting God's healing of that marriage. Make no mistake: God's will for every unhappy marriage isn't a fresh start with a new partner. That's the world's pattern. God's will is a fresh start, brought about by renewed thinking and transformed living that breaks the old habits—a fresh start with the wife or husband of our youth. If we follow the world's pattern and rush that marriage toward the precipice, we usurp God's authority—"Those whom God has joined together let no one put asunder," the traditional marriage service reads—and kill the patient before the Divine Healer can do his work.

On that December afternoon so long ago, Lory and I stood before my father in a church in Brooklyn, New York. We heard him speak of a time to come when the glow of our wedding festivities and the rapture of our honeymoon might have faded; a time when our own individual wills would assert themselves and our pride would isolate us. At the moment of newly-promised nuptial bliss, such hardness of heart seemed impossible, but he warned us nonetheless. As an antidote to the poison of self-centered pride and the alienating, destructive power of bitterness, my father recommended the words of St. Paul: "Be kind and compassionate to one another, forgiving each other, just as in Christ God forgave you" (Ephesians 4:32).

Reciprocal love, expressed as simple kindness, compassion, and forgiveness, is the balm that will heal every hurt. The source of that healing is the same forgiving grace by which we have been forgiven our sins. So must we forgive and be forgiven by those whom we once loved and can learn to love again.

When wife and husband return to their first love, they'll find their relationship as parents changing for the better. Children respond to love, and when they're surrounded by love—

not just for them but for everyone in the family—respect and accord will generally follow.

But such respect and accord must be mutual, not one-sided. Just as marriages must develop and nurture mutual respect, so too must the parent-child relationship. Husbands err if they expect their wives to respect them just because they're male. With children it's the same. Children don't necessarily respect their parents just because those parents are bigger and stronger, therefore somehow older and wiser. Parents earn respect by their actions. St. Paul cautioned the fathers particularly in Ephesus and Colosse against taking for granted their children's obedience and respect. "Fathers," he wrote, "do not exasperate your children" (Ephesians 6:4); "fathers, do not embitter your children, or they will become discouraged" (Colossians 3:21).

The word *exasperate* literally means "treat roughly." By our overbearing expectations, by our excessive demands, by our setting impossible standards, by our inconsistent discipline, by favoritism of one child over the other—by all these and more failings as parents, we can treat a child too roughly, thereby enraging the child to rebellious behavior. We can embitter and discourage the child.

But the opposite of "exasperate" isn't necessarily molly-coddling and pampering; it's a loving and caring insistence on "the training and instruction of the Lord" (Ephesians 6:4). Here again we have that reference to the *paideia* of the Lord, of which we've already spoken; but here too is the *nouthesia*, the correction and, if necessary, punishment that accompanies correction. In St. Paul's era, the Athenian schoolboy's learning included not only the academic subjects but also occasional corporal punishment administered with a standard little whip carried by the household slave who accompanied the boy to school each day. This whipping was the *nouthesia*, the admonition, the reminder that learning is serious business.

So today we as parents and grandparents must love and teach, love and instruct, love and rebuke, love and correct, love and punish when necessary. Otherwise, how will our children and grandchildren know we care?

Love for Friends

In all this emphasis upon love between family members, let's not overlook the love of friendship. How barren our lives would be without the affection and loyalty of a "best friend." Some of us are blessed from childhood with such lasting relationships; other friendships develop later as we move to a new locale, a new place of business, a new congregation.

God has blessed each of us with individual personalities; but he has also graced us with certain affinities, qualities that serve like magnets to attract others to us and us to them. These characteristics may be similarities of taste. They may also be opposite likes and dislikes which by their very differences help to complement a relationship.

Friendship, like marriage, relies on trust. It must never be taken for granted or abused. But even when one friend injures another and endangers their friendship, the true test of that friendship and its survival remains an obligation of the injured friend. For what does the apostle tell us in his great paean to reciprocal love?

> Love is patient, love is kind. It does not envy, it does not boast, it is not proud. It is not rude, it is not self-seeking, it is not easily angered, it keeps no record of wrongs. Love does not delight in evil but rejoices with the truth. It always protects, always trusts, always hopes, always perseveres (1 Corinthians 13:4-7).

So whether as husband and wife, as parent and child, or as friend and neighbor, the sign that we're acting like Christ will be our enduring love. In sum, "Love never fails" (1 Corinthians 13:8). Oh, to be that kind of faithful mate, that kind of devoted family member, that kind of reliable friend!

Chapter 11

The Beauty of Holiness

> wor-ship, *noun [ME* worshipe *worthiness,
> repute, respect, reverence paid to a diving
> being, fr. OE* weorthscipe *worthiness, re-
> pute, respect, fr.* weorth *worthy, worth* +
> -scipe *-ship]*
>   Webster's New Collegiate Dictionary

" "**G**od is spirit," Jesus of Nazareth told the Samaritan woman, "and his worshipers must worship in spirit and in truth" (John 4:24). What does this mean? Among many things, Jesus means that we must approach God in recognition of who God is—his character, his worth—then offer worship appropriate to the nature of God.

The British court system offers an example. In court the opposing attorneys wear robes and wigs and address the presiding judge as "Your Worship." Off the bench the judge may be a disreputable husband or a notorious drunk; but seated in his court, attired in his own robe and wig, and carrying the weight of English law in his decisions, that judge is deemed *worthy* of respect in appearance, speech, and manners. Furthermore, he has the power to enforce that respect.

135

Our own courts carry on the British custom to a more limited degree. Our attorneys don't dress like their British counterparts, but they do call the judge "Your Honor." Another thing: Have you noticed how the alleged thugs and hooligans who come into the court don't appear before the bench in their street clothes? They come in suit and tie— presumably for the first time since their last trial. Why don't they dress in jeans and T-shirt, their usual costume? The court demands respect, and they need to appear respectable and respectful.

EVANGELICAL WORSHIP IN DISREPAIR

Who is God? God is love, yes; God is also righteousness, justice, and truth. But above all, God is absolute holiness. Perhaps no single doctrine is in such disrepair in the evangelical subculture as is the doctrine of God's holiness, at least as represented by what passes for worship in our churches.

Informal Worship

In so many congregations on a Sunday morning we've exchanged the possible sterility of formal litany for the inevitable emptiness of disorder, whim, and utterance of whatever-comes-to-the-tip-of-the-tongue. We've been co-opted by the cult of spontaneity, the heresy of informality. We've replaced rigor and solemnity in worship with ease; we've elevated laxity to a virtue. We've sold the joy of dignity for the sake of weekend leisure. It shows in our dress, our preaching, and in our music.

Come with me to a Sunday morning representative of "worship" in many contemporary evangelical churches. The congregation arrives, for the most part, in whatever casual attire fits the climate—in Tucson or Irvine or Fort Lauderdale, the men are in slacks, golf shirts, topsiders; the women in pant suits at best; the youth in whatever they've chosen. It's all so laid-back and comfortable. After all, we're only going to church. Besides, doesn't the Bible say that "man looks at the outward appearance, but the LORD looks at the heart" (1 Samuel 16:7)? So who cares?

Of course, it's a different scene on Monday morning at work or Friday evening at the club or Saturday morning at the bridal brunch. There these same casual evangelicals will be clothed as serious executives and professionals or as members who take pride in their club or as wedding guests, dressed for the part. They'd never think of insulting Merrill Lynch or the club's board of governors or the bride's mother by showing up in anything less than what ironically used to be called "Sunday-go-to-meetin' " garb.

You don't have to be much of a sociologist to know that apparel indicates and often dictates attitudes. Consider for a moment the garage mechanic and the stock broker. When you take your Pontiac to have its transmission checked, do you want your mechanic to greet you in a tuxedo? When you go to check your portfolio with the brokerage house, do you want to be greeted by your broker in a pair of Bermuda shorts or a jump suit? Why not? Because in each case, proper attire represents the proper attitude toward getting the job done effectively. You want to see grease on your mechanic's overalls because you expect him to work on the greasy interior of your car's machinery. You want to see your broker dressed in a business suit because you expect her to take a highly businesslike approach to your investments. You don't want her at ease or playful about your finances.

If our God is sublimely holy, then our worship of him must be holy in order to be worthy. It's hard for us to be holy. We need all the help we can get. That's why it's important for us to take our worship seriously and do all we can to adorn it, starting with our own personal adornment. We need to take a bath, fix our hair, and put on our best clothes—not for God's sake but for ours! Because God is to be worshiped "acceptably with reverence and awe," as the writer to the Hebrews tells us (Hebrews 12:28).

Powerless Preaching

No doubt the principal reason our evangelical churches are deficient in reverence and awe for a holy God is that our evangelical subculture continues to be biblically illiterate and spiritually malnourished, fed on topical discussions and subjective experience, instead of a diet of a well-reasoned and articulate exposition of Scripture.

Whatever happened to preaching, real preaching? Powerful, sublimely uplifting, convicting preaching that points away from the preacher to the holiness of God? Not pulpit thumping or ranting; we still have plenty of that. Not lectures and book reviews, dull essays delivered like an exercise in Oral Interp 101. You can hear those too, sterile and academic, but oh so sophisticated.

Preaching is a gift given by the Holy Spirit, who is still in command of the distribution of God's gifts. But it seems that preaching is in shorter supply than it used to be. One of the causes for its present shortage may be the straightforward fact that, as our secular culture has become more and more visual, less and less verbal (image vs. idea, picture vs. word, film vs. book, television vs. radio), so the communication of thought by speeches, addresses, lectures, and sermons has also declined. We certainly see this to be true in political affairs. Lincoln and Douglas debated for hours at a time. In a parody of those debates, today's political candidates are given ninety seconds in which to make a pitch. Our modern attention span has been compressed to almost zero.

With the national slide in verbal communication as well as in reasoning skills, the evangelical subculture suffers the same loss. How will a preacher stir his congregation to act upon the Scripture's warning or trust its promise or respond to its challenge if his trumpet valves are stuck and give forth an uncertain sound—"Like, y' know, this is really neat! Hey, I'm excited!" Crippled by such powerlessness, his argument falters, incapable of summoning its listeners to submission and obedience to what the Bible teaches.

Ignorance of what the Bible says is epidemic throughout our evangelical subculture. Far worse is *ignoring* what the Bible says, disregarding its teachings and treating them with contempt. The secular world's pattern for today is "the right of private judgment." If I don't like what the Bible says on a certain issue—if it appears to condemn my secret sin—I don't have to feel bad about disregarding that particular precept. It just isn't truth for me! I find another way around the passage; or like Jehoiakim, king of Judah, I cut out of the scroll any text that offends me, throwing it into the fire (Jeremiah 36:23-24). Before long, the entire canon is consumed. Meanwhile, who's afraid of God's divine retribution?

At a time when professed evangelical believers are able to set aside biblical standards for Christian behavior, we must ask, "Have the words changed in a single generation? Does the New International Version permit something the King James Version did not? Or have our attitudes toward the authority of a holy God's commands altered?"

It's time to rid ourselves of any misrepresentation of God as a divine Caspar Milquetoast, a ludicrous depicting of God as an indulgent pushover. We need to read again the passage in Hebrews 12:28-29, summoning us to "worship God acceptably with reverence and awe, for our 'God is a consuming fire.' "

There's something unremitting about a fire. It scorches and burns everything in its path, regardless of worth or sentimental value. That's the inevitable accounting St. Paul warns us is coming on that day when we stand before God the Righteous Judge. God's burning holiness will turn to ashes our foolish offerings of wood, hay, and stubble—our TV ratings and platinum recordings and best-selling books; our church growth statistics and mass evangelism numbers and cross-cultural conversions. Even our gold must be tried out to have its dross burned away. How then can we presume to stand before the Lord of Creation, having dared to offer him anything less than the honor, the *worthship*, that is his due?

Artless Music

Which brings me to the third area of our disrespect in worship: the music that has subtly imposed itself upon evangelical Christianity, so-called "contemporary Christian music."

In the more primitive era of my youth, such music—or its then-current equivalent, boogie-woogie and swing—had no place in Christian worship. Oh, we had our nimble-fingered pianists, and how we loved to hear The Old-Fashioned Revival Hour's Rudy Atwood working at theme-and-variations on "Heavenly Sunshine"! Or the young Tedd Smith cranking out novel chords and arpeggios for "How Great Thou Art." But this was as far as we could go. As for serious music, Bach was too highbrow and almost every other composer seemed tainted by his supposed compromise with either the Vatican or Hollywood. So we sang instead only the staid hymns and peppy choruses, "Every Day with Jesus," "Safe Am I," "Christ for Me." We were never allowed to hum or sing or play or listen to popular music because it was so obviously "the devil's music."

How values have changed! In recent years, the *New York Times*—not generally reckoned to be a champion of things evangelical—has devoted space for feature articles dealing with the new music of Christianity. One headline reads, "Rock: No Longer 'Devil's Music'?" Music critic Robert Palmer writes,

> When rock-and-roll enjoyed its initial surge of popularity in the mid-50s, many fundamentalist Christians recoiled in horror. To them, rock's "savage rhythms,"

and the thinly concealed sexual double entendre of many rock-and-roll lyrics made it "the Devil's music.". . . . Rock and fundamentalist, or "born again," Christianity have become more and more closely entwined since the '50s. Gospel record labels like Word and Myrrh have had substantial success with albums of Christian material by performers whose styles are otherwise indistinguishable from contemporary rock-and-roll.

Another article states, "Christian Pop Is Gaining Fans," quoting recording executives on the huge sums—close to a half billion dollars—being made from record sales alone.

No doubt about it, "contemporary Christian music" is big business. But that's not the point. The questions to be asked are these: As music, is it worship? Is it biblically sound? Is it theologically orthodox? Is it spiritually nourishing? Much of the music I hear today in churches, at Christian schools and colleges and conferences, and on radio and television stations calling themselves "Christian" makes me wonder about some missing ingredients: integrity and spiritual maturity.

We've spoken in a previous chapter about Christian musicians themselves and their need for integrity and spiritual maturity in their lives and work; there's no further need to chastise them. Here I'm emphasizing our responsibilities as worshipers to insist upon integrity and spiritual maturity in public worship. For integrity means seeking wholeness, unity, consistency, continuity, and honesty in worship. It means careful, prayerful, thoughtful planning of all phases of public worship, setting a tone that's conducive to reverence and awe in the sanctuary—whether that be a cathedral nave or a rented high school gymnasium. This means attempting to coordinate the many private needs and petitions of individual worshipers within the elements of public expression—invocation, congregational and choral singing, personal and corporate confession, reading and proclamation of the Word, celebration of thanksgiving in tithes and offerings, celebration of communion by receiving the Eucharist, benediction—all as public praise to God.

In each aspect, music plays a central part. Music is the art most often referred to in the Bible, almost always in conjunction with worship and praise. Music is the pre-Creation means of discourse in the sublimest reaches of heaven, the conversation between the galaxies as "the morning stars sang together" (Job 38:7). It's the speech of angels given to human beings and will be our means of praise throughout eternity. The eighteenth century English poet Philip Skelton captures that vision:

> Ye choirs above, raise now to God
> An anthem loud and long
> That all the universe may hear
> And join the grateful song.
> Praise him, ye sun, who dwells unseen
> Amid transcendent light
> Where thy bright shining orb would seem
> A spot as dark as night.

Imagine music as praise to God! Not music as sentimental self-indulgence or music as emotional spillover or music as political rage, but music as adoration of the One who is the very Author of melody and harmony, the Originator of rhythm and meter.

To be a whole work of art in praise to God, music must cohere in form and content, in unity of theme, purpose, and style. If the music is song, then rhythm and meter, melody and harmony must mesh with the lyrics, the words being sung. Let me illustrate this point with a couple of deliberately awkward suggestions. First, let's sing the magnificent words of Psalm 107, "O give thanks unto the Lord"—but to the tune of "Old MacDonald Had a Farm." Ready?

> O give thanks unto the Lord—
> Ee-eye, Ee-eye, O!

Does the musical setting strike you as somehow ill-suited to the text? Or how about Psalm 23 in the words of the Scottish Psalter—but rather than one of the old hymnal tunes, "Crimond" or perhaps "Wiltshire," let's hear it to the rousing strains of the United States Marine Corps Hymn:

> The Lord's my shepherd; I'll not want;
> He makes me down to lie.

Semper Fidelis! I'm sure even the most tone-deaf reader can get the point of my parody. Judged by this same standard of aesthetic integrity—the blending of form and content to make a whole work of art—much of what we choose to sing from the catalog of contemporary Christian music isn't very far above the level of jingle or ditty. It ought to embarrass us to offer it to God as an example of our praise. I'm thinking in particular of those churches where the hymnal has been replaced by an overhead projector displaying so-called "Scripture songs," the grandeur of whose texts is trivialized by the tunes to which these glorious words are set. Good intentions, yes; but is this music? Is this praise to God?

Beyond issues of integrity are those relating to spiritual maturity. The principal metaphor of the New Testament is the analogy of the new birth, from which follows growth to maturity. This is the divine ideal. Sadly, however, what we all too often find in the evangelical church is that same immaturity St. Paul found in Corinth. Because of the Corinthians' prolonged infancy, the Apostle told them that they weren't yet ready for the strong meat they should have been able to assimilate. Instead, they were still to be fed on milk.

In these same terms, musically speaking, much of evangelical Christianity is still in its infantile stages; still being nursed, still sucking that vapid, tasteless formula, still slobbering over our jars of baby food. Or to use the analogy as it's expressed in the Letter to the Hebrews, we're still locked in to "the elementary teachings about Christ" (Hebrews 6:1); we're still lisping the ABCs of the gospel, still trying to master the two-times table.

Have you watched some people on a cafeteria line or at a buffet brunch? They look at the variety of foods displayed; then they choose something as dull as chopped steak, canned peas, and Jell-O pudding; or they select corn flakes and toast. They completely ignore the delicacies of the house, the specialties the chef has prepared. They never know what they're missing!

In the same way, God has a banquet of beef Wellington and roast pheasant for us to enjoy—a whole smorgasbord of delights for us to sample and enjoy and be nourished by. God has a vast library for us to peruse; God has all of calculus for us to play with. We don't have to go on, like children, ordering from the same menu; we don't have to remain in the nursery, clutching our toys. God invites us to grow up, to improve our taste, to throw away the junk food—or, at least, not to limit ourselves to that monotonous diet. God wants us to expand our acquaintance with his grace and glory. He'd like us, just for once, to pass by the sanctified hamburger and move over and up to some of his higher cuisine.

Make no mistake: Just as some foods are less nutritious than others, so some praise is inferior to other offerings, as Cain's was inferior to Abel's. Professor Donald P. Hustad of Southern Baptist Theological Seminary points out the inferiority of a recently popular chorus, "Let's Just Praise the Lord." In an article aptly titled "Let's Not Just Praise the Lord," Hustad writes that these words

> seem to express a casual approach to the holy service of worship. The problem may be with the word *just*—as in "Let's *just* sit down and have a cup of coffee."

Then Hustad recommends that

> those who expect worship to be more reasoned and

rational must patiently and lovingly introduce their
people to the deeper emotional resources of *words* that
will truly challenge and stimulate the imagination.

Hustad knows that spiritual maturity in music, as any-
where else in worship, is progressive: it leads from step to step,
developing as we grow in grace. To be mature means to
recognize our need for even further growth, as St. Paul said,
using one of his favorite athletic metaphors:

> Not that I have already obtained all this. . . . But one
> thing I do: Forgetting what is behind and straining
> toward what is ahead, I press on toward the goal to
> win the prize for which God has called me heaven-
> ward in Christ Jesus (Philippians 3:12-14).

Often when I speak in these terms, someone takes issue
with me by asking, "But isn't it all a matter of taste?" To this I
reply, "Yes, and God has excellent taste!" Then I try to recall
that God is also no snob, so that while we all struggle to learn
how best to bring our gifts to his service, God blesses even
some of our least worthy attempts at worship.

Worship is an art; it's also an obligation to love the Lord
with all my soul. An old tradition among sculptors holds that
every block of marble contains a statue or other work of art
struggling for freedom. The obligation of the sculptor is to
release that statue from its prison in the block of stone—to set
free the soul of the marble. So as apprentice artists, we come
before God the Master Artist and attempt to offer him our
works of praise. Horatius Bonar prays this prayer with us:

> In the still air the music lies unheard;
> In the rough marble beauty lies unseen.
> To wake the music and the beauty needs the Master's
>   touch,
> The Sculptor's chisel keen.

Great Master, touch me with thy hand;
Let not the music in me die.
Great Sculptor, hew and polish me;
    nor let there hidden, lost,
Thy form within me lie.

Spare not the stroke; do with me as thou wilt.
Let there be naught unfinished, broken, marred.
Complete, O Lord, thy purpose, that I may become
    thine image,
O my God and Lord.

It's a prayer of someone who has acknowledged the worthship of God and bowed in reverence before his majesty.

Chapter 12

Working for the Lord

> *Make Christ the only goal of your life.
> Dedicate to him all your enthusiasm, all
> your effort, your leisure as well as your
> business.*
>
> Desiderius Erasmus

*M*y wife and I live in a Long Island suburb of New York City, one of the bedroom communities in the vast metropolitan area. Each morning at 4:30, Monday through Friday, the first of eight Long Island Railroad trains chugs into the Stony Brook depot to carry its load of commuters to work in Manhattan or Brooklyn or Queens. Each afternoon, from 5:22 until 8:11 in the evening, another eight trains make their homebound stops.

Occasionally a business appointment summons me to join the regulars on one of these commuting trips. Perhaps it's the early hour or the mind-dulling inevitability of more than ninety minutes on the train; perhaps it's the weariness of too many trains over too many years. For whatever reason, few of my fellow passengers look happy about going to work. Their styrofoam coffee cups and morning newspapers in hand, these brave souls mount the cattle cars for another day at the warehouse, office, or store. For all the jollity of their banter with the conductor or their levity during the obligatory card game, there's not much pleasure in prospect as the train arrives at its destination. With the conductor's final station call, one can almost hear the daily commuters' prayer, "Lead us not into Penn Station."

Work as a Curse

Let's face it, for many people work is a curse. They look upon their jobs as a form of imprisonment. Hence the glamour of the weekend slogan, TGIF, "Thank God, it's Friday!" especially when a national holiday has been shifted to a Monday observance; or the attraction of management's suggestion of an expanded four-day work schedule to allow for an additional day of leisure; or the glamour of the distant but promised respite of a two-week vacation.

In some cases, the work itself has been permitted to become too demanding, too strenuous, and those who've given themselves utterly to that work have become addicted to work-for-work's-sake; we call them "workaholics." Often such people are searching for self-esteem. Unable to find it within themselves, they derive a sense of self-worth from the importance of their contribution to the job. So they inflate the most minor project until it assumes major proportions. C. Northcote Parkinson has satirized this phenomenon as "Parkinson's Law," which tells us that "work expands so as to fill the time available for its completion" and that "the thing to be done swells in importance and complexity in direct ratio with the time to be spent."

In other instances, the work is too boring, too mindless, for human dignity, and so becomes dispiriting. Henry David Thoreau described such work in his essay, "Life Without Principle,"

Most men would feel insulted if it were proposed to

employ them in throwing stones over a wall, and then in throwing them back, merely that they might earn their wages. But many are no more worthily employed now.

Still others are dissatisfied with their wages and benefits or with their working conditions; they go to work as if to mortal combat against management, whom they regard as the sworn enemy of the working class. Finally, there are some so cowed by authority, they adopt a servile stoop in deference to any representative of the employer, no matter how lowly in status.

So, with a despair born out of frustration, boredom, rage, servility—and, yes, indolence—the masses fill their forty hours per week. Only a minority do so with pride in accomplishment, with a sense of fulfillment, or even with a chauvinistic awareness that their productivity is being measured against foreign competitors. The burden of debt incurred by increasing consumer credit is all that sends most workers out of their houses each morning. Recently one of the most popular bumper stickers I've seen has been the take-off on the song of the Seven Dwarfs, "I owe, I owe, so off to work I go."

Work as Service

How different should be the Christian attitude toward work. For Christians are commanded to love the Lord with all our strength. Few workers know the joy of what Christians should understand to be their "calling" or *vocation*. The Scriptures assure us that every one of us has a place to fill in God's scheme of things; none of us is superfluous to God's plan. Furthermore, each of us is called to serve by the same Lord Jesus Christ who called Simon the fisherman and Levi the publican and Saul the pharisee of Tarsus; our calling is no less than theirs. It's a calling to follow him and serve as his faithful disciple.

Our discipleship itself is work. In fact, St. Paul describes the Christian experience in three comparative degrees relating to work. Writing to the Thessalonians, he commends them for "your work produced by faith, your labor prompted by love, and your endurance inspired by hope in our Lord Jesus Christ" (1 Thessalonians 1:3).

These three words—*work*, *labor*, and *endurance*—convey something of the intensifying nature of Christian discipleship which begins as an act of faith. The word St. Paul uses is *ergon*, from which we obtain the word "energy." Physicists tell us that any act or action, no matter how minimal, constitutes the use or exchange of energy; work of some sort takes place. Faith begins as an energizing act of belief. A commitment is made, an affirmation is declared, an offer is accepted, and the work of redemption is accomplished—the work of faith.

Beyond work lies labor, a more demanding use of energy. Here the Greek work is *kopos*. If *ergon* is any act requiring energy, *kopos* is grunt work: carrying a hod of bricks in ninety-degree heat, digging a ditch or stacking sandbags or doing the spring housecleaning—labor that requires getting your hands dirty and probably results in a sore back. St. Paul equates this kind of labor with evidence of *agapē*, labor made possible by Christian love: a willingness to perform the most menial task as an act of love.

But work and labor are nothing as measured against the third and highest degree of work: "endurance," the NIV's translation of *hupomonēs*. Here the text's connotation is persistence in the face of adversity, a willingness to grit your teeth and hang on to the end, the kind of tenacity that simply will not quit. St. Paul is describing the quality of constancy, determination, and fortitude required of the Christian—courage in spite of hardship. I think of Sir Winston Churchill's advice to boys at his old school. He glowered at them and said, "Never give up. Never give up. Never give up. Never, never, never give up."

Such endurance, however, demands more than a set of bulldog's teeth. There must be a reason for holding on, for refusing to give up or give in. For the Christian, that reason is hope—not some shallow kind of vague optimism or mere positive thinking but hope in the reality of God-in-Christ, the only cause for hope. The Bible teaches that believers in Jesus Christ have a reason for hope (1 Peter 3:15), secured by an unbreakable bond guaranteeing the faithfulness of God himself, a veritable anchor to the soul (Hebrews 6:16-19). This hope is a blessed anticipation (Titus 2:11-14); most of all, this hope is centered in a Person, "Christ Jesus our hope" (1 Timothy 1:1).

The call to discipleship isn't a call to leisure; it's a call to work, labor, and endurance. Furthermore, it isn't necessarily a call to some peculiarly pious endeavor. You don't have to be a pastor or missionary or Bible translator or church organist to work, labor and endure for Jesus Christ. Your work can be whatever God has given you to do—driving a truck, baking bread, coaching volleyball, designing computer programs, delivering the mail, vacuuming carpets, answering the telephone, caring for the family. For each one of us, there's a specific call to serve, a vocation to be filled, a service to be rendered as unto God.

I've witnessed this sense of vocation dramatically represented in one of the most intriguing parts of America, Sioux County in Northwest Iowa, home of Dutch immigrants and their descendants. It's an industrious community—a mixture of sprawling farms and light manufacturing—and a well-educated community, supporting its schools and colleges, Northwestern College in Orange City, Dordt College in Sioux Center. It's also a devoutly Christian region—one of the last remaining areas on this continent where Christendom is still flourishing. The influence of Reformation teaching and Covenant theology pervades even an after-luncheon speech before the local Lions' Club. But perhaps most striking are the attire and attitude of the Sioux County Dutch farmer in his field, in his barn, wherever he is at work. He customarily wears a hat and necktie while performing his chores, dressed for work as if for worship because he has been taught that work *is* worship.

Work as Worship

Work and worship. The biblical mandate, found first in Genesis 1 and 2, makes it clear that we're commissioned by God to be stewards of his Creation, to offer as a daily sacrifice in worship the work of our hands. A distorted view of life in Eden before the Fall romanticizes Adam and Eve into aimless layabouts who had nothing at all to do. Not so. Adam was expected to tend the garden, to care for his environment, in this way to participate in the ongoing work of Creation. We can hardly imagine that, while he did so, Adam's wife spent her days admiring herself in a reflecting pond. Together they rearranged the floral plantings and trimmed the hedges—of course, there were no weeds to pull—and did all those things for which we never seem to have enough time.

Adam and Eve worked in Eden, and presumably that work brought them joy. Only after rebellion did God's curse turn Adam's work into toil:

> "Cursed is the ground because of you;
>   through painful toil you will eat of it
>   all the days of your life.
> . . . .
> By the sweat of your brow
>   you will eat your food
> until you return to the ground"
> (Genesis 3:17, 19).

But even after work had become toilsome, God blessed the worker with an added gift: the thrill of satisfaction with a job well done.

Work as God's Gift

Work is a blessing. If you doubt this, think for a moment of two classes of non-workers: the unemployed and the super-annuated. To the unemployed, their inability to find or obtain a position of steady employment represents more than a loss of earning power; it also represents a loss of self-esteem, a loss of family pride, a loss of community contribution, a loss to the gross national product. Social workers tell us that an unemployed husband in particular is a time bomb waiting to explode—a potential abuser of his wife and children—so enraged by his own economic impotence, he lashes out in physical violence as his only means of self-assertion.

Some retired persons also show signs that they miss the blessing of work. Many, of course, retire to productive lives full of alternative activity and enterprise; they tell the truth when they profess never to have taken a backward look at the job left behind. But for others, particularly those for whom the job represented status and power, the void left when their work is taken from them engulfs their lives. They literally pine away for want of something productive to do. The mortality rate among retired middle-level executives is highest in the first two years of retirement; apparently, they die of boredom.

Yes, work is one of God's gifts to the human race. So the opportunity to do our work needs to be accepted with gratitude. I've developed a personal prayer of thanksgiving which I pray almost every day: "Thank you, Lord, for life, for love, for work and the strength to do it, for play and the sense to enjoy it." It's a simple prayer that covers my day-by-day experience: life and the health that sustains it; love and the persons on whose love I depend; work and the fulfillment it brings; play and the respite it affords.

Excellence in Work

But I also need to put legs under that prayer; no formula will do. My profession of gratitude to God rises and assumes a concrete shape only as I live out that gratitude in loving and working and playing. My work becomes worship only when it's done wholeheartedly and to the best of my ability. "Whatever your hand finds to do," the Teacher of wisdom declares, "do it with all your might" (Ecclesiastes 9:10). My work becomes an offering worthy to be presented to God only when it's performed with joy. Anything less than my best effort, anything less than joyful service, will never earn God's "Well done!"

To receive God's approval, our work must be nothing short of excellent. That's what matters: Not how I feel about my work but how God evaluates its excellence. One of the most overused and undervalued words in our vocabulary is this fine word *excellence*. So often the word appears as part of advertising hyperbole, as a come-on to lure us toward what turns out to be no more than ordinary, mundane, trivial. Few of us know what excellence means anymore; most of us have come to recognize excellence as a cliché, if not an outright misrepresentation. Still, the search for excellence goes on.

Sometimes when we find it difficult to get a grasp on the meaning of an abstraction like excellence, it helps to look at its opposite. Emerson reminded us that there's often some value in looking at the world upside-down, with your head between your legs. So, if we want to know what excellence is, we may have to look at what it most certainly isn't.

Excellence isn't "minimal competency," that degrading term suggesting that we'll settle for a level of performance that's just barely good enough. Think of it this way: How would you like to fly with an airline whose pilots are no more than minimally competent? How would you like to know that your surgeon had passed his board exams with a grade indicating minimal competence? No, merely "good enough" is never good enough.

Neither is "mediocrity." Some years ago, a federal commission reported on the ruinous state of education in America, describing "a nation at risk" of being overwhelmed by "a rising tide of mediocrity." What an image! America awash in mediocrity, facing economic and cultural disintegration because of half-heartedness, half-fulfillment, half-effort. Because that's what mediocrity denotes: It comes from two Latin words meaning "halfway up a stony mountain."

What's more, mediocrity isn't just an educational problem or a corporate problem or a national problem; it's a personal problem. Schools aren't mediocre; but if administrators and teachers and students can be half-hearted about their work, the school fails to achieve excellence. Businesses aren't mediocre; but when management and labor give only half-effort to the production of goods and services, the corporation falls short of excellence. Marriages and homes aren't mediocre; but if husbands and wives, parents and children, are guilty of less than full commitment to their responsibilities to each other, the family suffers.

Work as Stewardship

But what, then, is excellence? To keep it as simple as possible, excellence is making the most of what we've been given. Excellence is stewardship. Certainly this is the teaching implicit in the parable of the three stewards in Matthew 25. God is the giver of every good and every perfect gift; as recipients of those gifts, we're to invest those gifts and make them flourish then return the proceeds as evidence of our stewardship. To the degree that we improve on our original bequest, we earn the Father's commendation for work well done. To that same degree, our work approaches the divine standard of excellence, for which there can be no substitute.

Unless I'm willing—no, more than that, unless I'm eager—to learn more about the Scriptures and their application to my living like a Christian, I contribute to the mediocrity rife throughout evangelical Christianity. Unless I struggle to master the skills of my calling—whatever it may be—I face the certainty of hearing God's ultimate rebuke. My focus must be on what pleases God; that, after all, is the final objective in work, as St. Paul told the slaves in the Colossian church:

> Slaves, obey your earthly masters in everything; and do it, not only when their eye is on you and to win their favor, but with sincerity of heart and reverence

for the Lord. Whatever you do, work at it with all your heart, as working for the Lord, not for men, since you know that you will receive an inheritance from the Lord as a reward. It is the Lord Christ you are serving (Colossians 3:22-24).

God has a higher call for all of us, a call to excellence, a call to love him with all—not some, not half, but all—our strength.

Chapter 13

God's Game of Hide-and-Seek

> *What the world expects of Christians is that Christians should speak out, loud and clear, in such a way that never a doubt, never the slightest doubt, could rise in the heart of the simplest man.*
>
> Albert Camus

*T*o begin answering Charles M. Sheldon's question, "What would Jesus do?" we must translate our profession of faith in the Lordship of Jesus Christ into everyday terms. We must experience the reality of God's grace in our common living.

THE HIDDENNESS OF GOD

For many people, caught in the maelstrom of secular culture or living on the edge of the Judeo-Christian value system, their major barrier to accepting the validity of the gospel remains the seeming hidden nature of God. "If only God would reveal himself," they lament, "if only God would speak directly to me." One of the most seductive elements of today's charismatic preachers—particularly the flamboyant television evangelists—has been their claim to possess disclosures of special revelation that break through the inscrutable hiddenness of God.

The great French mathematician and Christian humanist Blaise Pascal understood the nature of God's reality. In his collection of mystical thoughts called *Pensées*, Pascal explains that "men are in darkness and estranged from God." The reason for this separation is "that he has hidden himself from their knowledge, that this is in fact the name which he gives himself in the Scriptures, *Deus absconditus*," which means "the hidden God." Yet Pascal goes on to argue that men would do better if, "instead of complaining that God had hidden himself, you will give him thanks for having revealed so much of himself."

One of my favorite poems by Emily Dickinson poses this same problem. Plagued by alternating belief and doubt, the agnostic Dickinson writes of God's apparent choice to play hide-and-seek with his Creation.

> I know that He exists.
> Somewhere—in Silence—
> He has hid his rare life
> From our gross eyes.
>
> 'Tis an instant's play.
> 'Tis a fond Ambush—
> Just to make Bliss
> Earn her own surprise.
>
> But—should the play
> Prove piercing earnest—
> Should the glee—glaze—
> In Death's—stiff—stare
>
> Would not the fun
> Look too expensive!
> Would not the jest—
> Have crawled too far!

According to the poet, God's inscrutable plan to hide and remain hidden until found runs a mortal risk. Suppose that, like Dickinson herself, the seeker takes the game seriously but to no avail? Suppose the hidden God is never found?

All discussion about what it means to think and act like a Christian in the present secular culture comes down to one point: Is God really hidden in the world we live in? If so, why? and where and by whom may he be found? If not, where then may he be seen clearly and unmistakably by all? Where does God's manifestation of himself intersect with the biblical concept of a "Deus absconditus," to adopt Pascal's phrase?

According to Genesis, God was known to Adam and Eve, communing with them daily, walking in the garden in the cool of the day. But they disobeyed, bringing about the Fall and its consequences, the first of which was their shameful need to hide themselves from God. As part of the aftermath of the Fall—some theologians would say, in retaliation for Adam and Eve's hiding themselves from God—God has cut off his common disclosure of himself, choosing to hide himself from humanity. So Carl Michalson wrote that "it is God's way of life to be hidden. He is *ex officio* hidden. Hiddenness is intrinsic to his nature as God."

The Disclosure of God in Christ

In the view of some theologians, God's hiddenness is a permanent condition; he is veiled in holiness too supernal to penetrate. For them, the very idea of a God who is not hidden is too anthropomorphic, too much like the Hindu avatars. Such rejection of a revealed God obtains its presumed biblical support from St. Paul's several references to the mystery or secret of God kept from open disclosure. But evangelicals differ from these theologians in our insistence on reading to the end of Paul's statements: "the mystery hidden for long ages past, *but now revealed and made known*" (Romans 16:25-26), and "*he made known to us the mystery* of his will according to his good pleasure, which he purposed in Christ" (Ephesians 1:9).

By accepting the complete testimony of the Scriptures as true, an evangelical must qualify the absolute hiddenness of God as a theological tenet because that notion of total hiddenness contradicts St. Paul's declaration to the Colossians, that Jesus of Nazareth is "the image ["the exact representation"] of the invisible God" (Colossians 1:15). If so, then in Christ, God is no longer utterly invisible, hence no longer utterly hidden. To go on indiscriminately referring to "the hiddenness of God" is to deny that God has already disclosed himself by his names and acts; to deny that God has chosen to reveal himself in the person of Jesus Christ; and to deny that the Lord of the universe is, in Carl F. H. Henry's phrase, "God who speaks and shows."

In sum, to speak uncritically of "the hiddenness of God" and mean theologically that there is no personal revelation of God to man is to reject the most elemental assertion of Christianity, that "God was in Christ" (2 Corinthians 5:19, KJV).

But if, theologically speaking, the revelation of God-in-Christ is no longer cryptic, no longer what St. Paul calls "God's secret wisdom, a wisdom that has been hidden" (1 Corinthians 2:7), is there not a sense, existentially speaking, in which God does remain hidden?

Certainly, in knowing Jesus Christ, we expect to find God among us in acts of devotion and worship: "Where two or three are gathered in my name . . ." and so on. God is always present wherever there is truth, wherever wisdom and beauty reside, wherever "the Good" of ancient philosophers is known. But now the question arises: Where else may God be found?

If God hides at all, does he hide only to disclose himself when and where we may least expect to find him? Indeed, may not God be found hiding even in falsehood, ignorance, and ugliness—within the very opposite of "the Good"? However incongruous this seems, perhaps the paradox may be stated in these terms: When Satan lies about the faithfulness of God, he lies because he fears the truth he knows. His lie, therefore, is Satan's own twisted affirmation that God *is* faithful.

Perhaps Harvey Cox is right when he avers that "God also survives among philosophers intent on denying his existence. They seem to know, at least, what it is whose existence they are denying." Another way of making the same point is this: Atheistic ranting is the single strongest argument in favor of the existence of God. One doesn't need to combat an enemy who isn't there. Organized and institutionalized atheism, therefore, is a tacit concession to the fact of an Enemy's threat. Madalyn Murray O'Hair is kept in business by the very fact of her militant atheism's futility at eradicating the ineradicable. God refuses to disappear, no matter how stridently the atheist protests. Thus, the major reason for Satan's lie, for the atheist's passionate denial, is a nagging fear that God will one day choose to come out of all hiding, revealing himself in cosmic sovereignty.

It seems apparent, therefore, that there is this other respect in which speaking about "the hiddenness of God" is both kerygmatically precise and evangelistically appropriate— true to the core of meaning at the heart of the Good News. Justin Martyr, Augustine of Hippo, and the Christian humanists recognized the immediacy of God's presence behind the veil of pagan literature, heathen temples, and deified human virtues or acts of nature—hidden, as Erasmus said, in "all studies, philosophy, rhetoric."

But that was before the collapse of Christendom. What about God's presence or absence in our age? Is God to be found at the end of the twentieth century? In the cultures of Western civilization? Within the Marxist bloc? In the nations of the Third World? And if so, where? Can God be found in history, in education, in social structures, in scientific research, in art, in industry? Is John Wiley Nelson right in entitling his book *Your God Is Alive and Well and Appearing in Popular Culture*?

CATCHING SIGHT OF GOD

To attempt an answer to these questions, I invite you to accompany my wife Lory and me on a weekend in New York City. The occasion is our thirtieth wedding anniversary. If your primary acquaintance with The Big Apple derives only from television impressions, let me assure you of two things. First, New York is far worse than you imagine. Its degradation, its political corruption, its materialism, its secular preoccupation with fad and fancy, exceed anything to be perceived by way of a TV rerun. Second, New York is far better than you may have feared, for in spite of sin and all its rot, the light of hope in Christ continues to glimmer and, in some places, even to shine brightly. St. Paul knew such a secular metropolis when he wrote to the Romans from Corinth, "But where sin increased, grace increased all the more" (Romans 5:20). That same grace is the theme of God's game of hide-and-seek.

It's the weekend before Christmas. Our plans are to celebrate our anniversary by spending Thursday night through Sunday afternoon at the Waldorf-Astoria Hotel on Park Avenue. As we arrive on that elegant boulevard, we encounter the garbage-infested streets of Manhattan. It's been seventeen days since the private carters and their drivers quarreled, resulting in a strike. Piles of plastic bags rise to mountains ten feet high and spill out in unspeakable filth. As it happens, this very afternoon the strike has been settled, but as yet no clean-up has begun. The mask of decency and civility, we discover, is no thicker than a heavy-duty trash bag. Yet we count it a notable act of God's common grace that this labor dispute occurred in subfreezing temperatures rather than in the middle of July!

But also on Park Avenue, an annual New York phenomenon greets us. Looming over the street stands the Helmsley Building, its office windows lit to form a giant cross. These windows will illumine the darkness of Park Avenue throughout the Advent and Christmas season, then again during the week from Palm Sunday until Easter.

After checking into our hotel, we leave for our celebratory dinner at the New York Athletic Club, where thirty years before we first dined as newlyweds. In a splendid dining room overlooking Central Park, we enjoy the bounties of food and drink, the specific reminiscences of our wedding day, the joyous memories of our first love-making. Our meal concluded, we walk without fear the mile back to the Waldorf, carefully avoiding the refuse piles and the rats feeding on them.

We've chosen to walk in order to enjoy the great landmarks of Fifth Avenue—the decorated windows of famous stores, the floral arrays in the great churches, and finally the angelic choir and giant tree at Rockefeller Center. Christmas in New York is a series of contrasts more sharply drawn, perhaps, than in Tulsa, Lynchburg, or Garden Grove—or even Orange City, Iowa—precisely because here in Gotham, the very stronghold of satanic delusion, truth keeps breaking through in all its relentless power.

As we walk through the sub-freezing streets, we're stunned by the sight of several bodies curled fetus-like in doorways or on sidewalk grates. The homeless—some vagrants by choice, some victims of neglect—underscore in either case a wrenching contrast to our middle-class security and occasional luxury. There, but for the grace of God, might be one of us. The mayor of the city has decreed that the police must compel all homeless persons to accept shelter for their own good. But the American Civil Liberties Union has obtained a restraining order on behalf of the street people, contending that they must be free to choose or reject shelter. Even as we pass, a squad car and van of police officers are unsuccessfully urging a bag lady to leave her accustomed spot near a heating vent.

Discussing the case—no longer a legal abstraction but vivid before our eyes—its theological parallel strikes home: Unlike the mayor, God limits himself from compelling anyone to accept his offer of redemption. His grace must draw the homeless to himself. The woman waves away the helpless policemen, and we shiver at the thought of the night awaiting her.

Friday morning dawns with the brightness of a crisp December day. From midnight on, the garbage collectors have been at work. Their goal is to have the streets clean again by Christmas, and from our sixteenth floor window I look out upon the disappearance of last night's pollution. Yet for all their renewed industry, these sanitation engineers can hardly eradicate the noxious stench that lingers as a reminder of strife on earth and ill will between them and their employers.

The morning newspaper at our door announces the death of two street people, including a woman found frozen on nearby 50th Street.

We leave our room for breakfast and find ourselves in a swarm of conventioneers from the American Psychotherapy Association. In the crowded hotel restaurant, we are seated cheek-by-jowl next to three badge wearers whose cigarette smoke and conversation intrude upon our eggs Benedict. They are a husband and wife with a female acquaintance, all of them psycho- therapists. The third party is going through a divorce; she speaks of her consternation and surprise at how her feelings keep interfering with what she had expected to be a purely rational, routine event—a minor surgical procedure—divesting herself of an unpleasant relationship.

For her apparent comfort, the wife tells her friend of an experience she'd had last evening. Her former husband, evidently another psychotherapist, had entered a room and joined a group in which she was standing. "He fastened his eyes on everyone—no minimal scanning at all—and spoke intently to everyone in the circle but me. He completely ignored the fact that I was present. When he left, it occurred to me that I'd spent eleven years married to that jerk!" To which her present husband adds his clinical wisdom: "Yes, there's pain to a divorce, a sense of loss. I regret the loss of time, the wasted years I spent with my first wife."

Lory and I gulp our coffee and leave before this cynicism can seep any further into our day. We're off to finish our Christmas shopping for our grandchildren. We try the nearby stores—Saks' Fifth Avenue and F. A. O. Schwarz—then go across town to Bloomingdale's, whose entire ground floor seems given over to scents and perfumes, the self-indulgence of preserving all the outward signs of physical attractiveness with little apparent reference to inward beauty. Homosexual couples are among the most frantically eager customers. The alabaster jar . . . "Drop, drop, slow tears."

En route to Bloomingdale's toy department we pass a notions counter where eccentric items are for sale, including a black-and-white aerosol can labeled "Guilt Away," from Corn-Berg Labs of Bellingham, Washington. It claims "spray on relief from guilt." Once priced at $5.00, this novelty appears not to have caught on and is now reduced to $2.50. Still no one seems to be buying it, even at this mark-down. Either Bloomingdale's patrons know that guilt lies deeper than aerosol sprays can penetrate or else these shoppers are indifferent to the weak humor.

Unable to find the specific toy we seek, we stop for a refreshing tankard of hot chocolate before taking the subway a few stops to Herald Square and Macy's department store. Only my long familiarity with the New York City Transit System enables us to get off at the right station because every window in our subway car has been blackened by thick paint, the initials and identifying symbols of vandals wielding spray cans. Once Simon and Garfunkel romanticized this nuisance, claiming that "the words of the prophets are written on the subway walls." Now, however, our underground transportation, marred by urban scrawl, may be the single most visible testimony against an era of catastrophic permissiveness at home and school, in the halls of legislatures and in courtrooms. This brief ride is the most depressing experience of the day.

But upon arriving at Macy's Toyland, where thirty-five years earlier I served as one of Santa's Helpers, each of us is hugged by Yogi Bear and aided by genuinely helpful sales-people. Their personal concern overrides sheer busyness. They take time to listen to our request, explaining the differences between one toy and another, offering to open a box and show its contents. We leave with our purchase, reassured that crass commerce hasn't yet entirely suppressed the Christmas Spirit.

By this time, the afternoon has slipped away, and we must return to our hotel to prepare for a concert we plan to attend. Dave Brubeck is to appear as composer-pianist in a production of his cantata, "La Fiesta de la Posada," at Fifth Avenue Presbyterian Church. As long as I can remember, I've been an admirer of Brubeck's improvisational genius; his 1950s recordings were a quantum leap over every other category of progressive jazz. Now, with his wife Iola's text, Brubeck has told the Christmas story in his own inimitable style. Every riff and curlicue, every meshing chord and modulation, pleases me.

But I'm not prepared for the soul-thrilling merging of exultant music with gospel narrative and original lyrics expressing faith.

> God's love made visible. Incomprehensible!
> He is invincible!
> His love shall reign!
>
> God gave His Son to us to dwell as one of us.
> His blessing unto us!
> His love shall reign!
>
> To Him all honor bring, heaven and earth will sing,
> Praising our Lord and King!
> His love shall reign!*

---

* From the cantata "La Fiesta de la Posada," music by Dave Brubeck; text by Iola Brubeck. © Copyright 1976, St. Francis Music Co. and Malcolm Music, Ltd.; Delaware Water Gap, PA 18327. All rights reserved. Used with permission.

Sitting in the church listening to this music, I now understand why I've been troubled throughout this season—and for
many Christmas seasons past—each time I've heard the popular ditty, "Have Yourself a Merry Little Christmas." The
sentiment may be pretty, but the expression is close to blas-
phemous. It's the diminutive word that galls me. Of course, it
aims at cuteness: everything "little" is cute. Yet the mindless
diminution of the event and all it signifies turns that expression
of cuteness into sacrilege. It's the same as the Doobie Brothers
once singing "Jesus is Just Alright with Me" or thoughtless
professed believers crooning sentimental slush like "Heavenly
Father, I Appreciate You." Where is the sense of God's
sovereign majesty? Where is our reverential awe? The Bru-
becks have found it and expressed it in their lyrics and jazz
idiom.

We return to the Waldorf for a late supper in much the
same spirit as the shepherds of old, glorifying and praising God
for all we have seen this day.

Saturday is again brilliantly sunny but freezing. Our
shopping concluded, we are to spend this day in museums and
theaters. After a breakfast of fresh croissants and coffee—
surely two of God's most gracious provisions!—we head toward the Metropolitan Museum of Art, almost two miles north.

Because the Met is too vast for more than selective
browsing, we've chosen to concentrate on the exhibition in the
American wing. But first, the famous Metropolitan Christmas
tree and its Nativity Scene. Figurines depict angels, shepherds,
Wise Men, animals, workmen, children, the Mother and Child
and Joseph; high above on the vaulted ceiling, the Star. This
sight alone is worth the price of admission.

From there we wander the corridors, gazing at the works
of American masters—Stuart, Peale, Cole, Homer, Eakins,
Bierstadt, Cassat, Whistler, Hopper, and the rest of the American pantheon. In one room are two paintings by a Stony Brook
native son, the nineteenth-century genre artist William Sidney

Mount. One of these depicts an ordinary Long Island farm house still standing close to our home. It's a reminder that art ennobles even the most humble subjects; art transforms the most common domestic dwelling into the grandeur of timelessness by means of the artist's vision shared with his audience. It's also a reminder that art is God's gift to both the painter and those who view his work.

We plan a late-afternoon movie to be followed by dinner. The theater is a mile away, yet in spite of the cold we choose a brisk walk. On our way down Madison Avenue, past the private art galleries and boutiques, we pass a luncheonette called the Pilgrim Restaurant. An unusual sign in its window catches my attention:

> NEED CHANGE? WE'RE GLAD TO MAKE CHANGE FOR YOUR PHONE CALL OR BUS FARE. NO PURCHASE NECESSARY. HAVE A GOOD DAY!

The movie we've chosen is *The Trip to Bountiful*, starring the late Geraldine Page in her Academy-award-winning performance. She plays the role of Carrie Watts, an elderly woman forced to live with her failed son Ludie and his waspish wife Jessie Mae. Carrie Watts has only two sources of strength, her deeply-rooted Christian faith and her indomitable desire to return once more to her childhood home in Bountiful, Texas.

She recites her memorized Bible verses and hums her hymns to give her courage in the face of her daughter-in-law's animosity and self-centeredness. The musical score of this film has been composed by a friend, J. A. C. Redford, himself a recent convert. He builds his score upon the base of the old evangelistic song, "Softly and Tenderly Jesus is Calling," sung by the crystalline voice of Cynthia Clawson.

In the climactic scene of the move, Carrie Watts reaches out in an act that is clearly intended to portray *agapē* toward her pagan daughter-in-law. The gesture is simple, but the moment becomes riveting. The Manhattan theater in which we view this film is one of the popular venues for entertainment, catering to its urban sophisticates. The aroma of marijuana drifts down from the balcony smoking zone.

But as Geraldine Page speaks and sings her character's words of faith in God, her trust in Jesus Christ, all breathing seems to cease, all motion freezes in stop-film. The mention of God and Christ are not unfamiliar in this theater, where profanity is an accepted reality. What can it mean, that a film honored around the world and hailed by major movie critics, witnesses for Jesus Christ? How can this be? A film that is "Christian" without having been produced by believers? A film that *shows* rather than *tells*? Amazing grace!

From the movie we return to our hotel to prepare for dinner at a favorite steak house. The early evening news on television includes the ongoing story of strife surrounding an Episcopal parish, St. Bartholomew's Church, adjacent to our hotel. The rector wishes to construct a skyscraper above the parish hall. His parish is divided; the City of New York has entered the controversy. We have planned to attend worship services there on Sunday morning. Listening to the news telecast, one wonders whether St. Bart's is a house of prayer or a den of thieves.

Our restaurant of choice is Christ Cella, whose magazine advertising reads, "Quite simply, superb food." If anything, the ad proves to be an understatement. The combination of ambiance, excellent service, and delectable cuisine turns a meal into an event, a cause for celebration, yet another moment of grace. We float rather than walk back to our hotel.

Before retiring, I turn on the television set and watch the final moments of Rona Barrett's interview with Mary Tyler Moore. The interviewer asks the actress to account for how she's been able to cope with personal tragedies—a divorce after many years of marriage, followed by the irony of her own son's mysterious death while she was playing a role of a mother grieving over her son's suicide. Mary Tyler Moore ponders the question, bites her lip, and says, "I have no religious faith to call on. I guess I'm just what you call a survivor; I survive."

I flip the channel and discover a late-night rebroadcast of the phenomenal film *Chariots of Fire*, the story of Eric Liddell, whose commitment to Jesus Christ led him from an Olympic gold medal to martyrdom in China. Although I've seen this movie numerous times, watching its message again lifts me beyond the despairing words of Mary Tyler Moore.

Our final morning in New York City is the Fourth Sunday in Advent, the Sunday before Christmas Day. We cross 50th Street and enter St. Bartholomew's Church for the celebration of Holy Communion, followed by the traditional Service of Lessons and Carols. Accustomed to our tiny country church, we're almost lost in the Byzantine immensity of this place, but we're soon aware that God himself is present in the Bread and Wine, in the Word and Carols. During the offertory, the embattled rector, Thomas D. Bowers, leads us all in singing "Go Tell It on the Mountain." After two choruses, he says, "Sing it a third time to wake all those still sleeping in the Waldorf!"

After brunch, we check out of the hotel and head for home, fifty miles east on Long Island. As we drive, I keep one ear tuned to the radio play-by-play of a New York Jets football game, aware that Don Fonseca, my friend and colleague at The Stony Brook School, has led the pregame chapel service for players, coaches, and their families. I realize that Eric Liddell, the All-Scotland rugby star turned Olympic sprinter, would not have been present at such a service, for his conscience would not have condoned his competing on Sundays; I acknowledge that others today may have the same scruples. But I also rejoice that, in every professional sport and on almost every team, athletes come together with their teammates in worship, knowing that—as Eric Liddell said—when they play to the best of their divinely-given talent, it pleases God.

Ahead of us on the Long Island Expressway is a battered Volkswagen van adorned with many window decals—a dove, a fish, a television program's logotype—and these bumper stickers:

GOD'S LAST NAME ISN'T DAMMIT!

GOD SAID IT, I BELIEVE IT, THAT SETTLES IT!

IN CASE OF RAPTURE, THIS VEHICLE WILL BE UNOCCUPIED.

Making Known the Grace of God

Driving the final few moments to Stony Brook and home, I'm thinking of what Albert Camus told a group of Roman Catholics in 1948:

> What the world expects of Christians is that Christians should speak out loud and clear . . . in such a way that never a doubt, never the slightest doubt, could rise in the heart of the simplest man.

What's my obligation as a Christian who lives *in* but not *of* the world? Isn't it to struggle toward an understanding of this great enigma: First, that God is indeed hidden and waiting to be discovered in every nook and corner of our culture. Nowhere is the presence of this surprising God more certainly confirmed than by his quietly and unobtrusively working even through the art of a skeptic like Camus. But, also, that when we fully discover who Jesus of Nazareth really is, we surely find that we're looking straight into the face of God himself—the very God who has "made his light shine in our hearts to give us the light of the knowledge of the glory of God in the face of Christ" (2 Corinthians 4:6).

By coming to know that Jesus of Nazareth is "the Christ, the Son of the living God," the paradoxical hiddenness of God is forever resolved by personal seeking-and-finding.

Here, then, is our responsibility as Christians: To make known the grace of God to those for whom his revelation in

Jesus Christ remains a mystery. For if each one of us accepted Albert Camus' challenge to "speak out loud and clear," not only with our lips but in our lives, how long would God remain hidden in our culture? How long before the Christ who wept over Jerusalem and who still weeps over every metropolis and hamlet in this world would, through our work and witness, "tread the city's streets again"?